OF *Christmases*
LONG, LONG AGO

OF *Christmases* LONG, LONG AGO

Surprising Traditions from Christmas Past

BRIAN EARL

Original Illustrations by Dorothy Siemens
Foreword by Gerry Bowler, PhD

LYONS PRESS

Essex, Connecticut

LYONS PRESS

An imprint of The Globe Pequot Publishing Group
64 South Main Street
Essex, CT 06426
www.lyonspress.com

Copyright © 2025 by Brian Earl

All rights reserved. No part of this book may be reproduced in any form or by any electronic or mechanical means, including information storage and retrieval systems, without written permission from the publisher, except by a reviewer who may quote passages in a review.

British Library Cataloguing in Publication Information Available

Library of Congress Cataloging-in-Publication Data

Names: Earl, Brian, 1974– author. | Siemens, Dorothy, illustrator.
Title: Of Christmases long, long ago : surprising traditions from Christmas past / Brian Earl ; Original Illustrations by Dorothy Siemens ; Foreword by Gerry Bowler, PhD.
Description: Essex, Connecticut : Lyons Press, [2025] | Summary: "For a celebration as old as Christmas, it's no surprise that many traditions have come and gone—what often is a surprise is just what some of those traditions were. This book reveals these traditions and will appeal to anyone whose Christmas spirit includes a healthy dose of curiosity"— Provided by publisher.
Identifiers: LCCN 2024045568 (print) | LCCN 2024045569 (ebook) | ISBN 9781493089659 (cloth) | ISBN 9781493089666 (epub)
Subjects: LCSH: Christmas—History. | Winter festivals.
Classification: LCC GT4985 .E175 2025 (print) | LCC GT4985 (ebook) | DDC 394.2663—dc23/eng/20241227
LC record available at https://lccn.loc.gov/2024045568
LC ebook record available at https://lccn.loc.gov/2024045569

♾️™ The paper used in this publication meets the minimum requirements of American National Standard for Information Sciences—Permanence of Paper for Printed Library Materials, ANSI/NISO Z39.48-1992

For Christine and Dashiell
"Good night, cinnamon–amon–amon!"

Contents

Foreword ix
Introduction .1

PART 1: SOCIAL INVERSION 9
Chapter 1: Cross-Dressing. 11
Chapter 2: The Boy Bishop 17
Chapter 3: The Feast of Fools 21
Chapter 4: The Bean King 27

PART 2: PARTIES AND FEASTS 31
Chapter 5: The Lord of Misrule 33
Chapter 6: Masking 37
Chapter 7: Dangerous Games 41
Chapter 8: Gross Foods 45

PART 3: RAUCOUS REVELS 49
Chapter 9: Callithumpian Parades. 51
Chapter 10: A "Breech" of Christmas Spirit . . . 55
Chapter 11: Holly Beating. 61
Chapter 12: Blowing the Christmas Pudding . . . 67

PART 4: MONEY AND CHARITY 73
Chapter 13: Begging Visits. 75
Chapter 14: Saving at the Pub 83
Chapter 15: Wren Day 87

PART 5: KEEPING HOUSE 93
Chapter 16: Undecking the Halls 95
Chapter 17: First-Footing 99

PART 6: GIFT BRINGERS. 103
Chapter 18: The Saint's Surly Servants 105
Chapter 19: Baby Jesus, Gift Bringer 111
Chapter 20: Grandfather Frost. 117

PART 7: THE WILD SIDE 127
Chapter 21: Monsters 129
Chapter 22: The Mari Lwyd 135
Chapter 23: Skeklers 141
Chapter 24: The Broad 147
Chapter 25: Ghost Stories 153

Acknowledgments 167
About the Author and Illustrator 169

Foreword

Christmas is the biggest thing there is. No international sporting event, stadium rock tour, election campaign, social media craze, or global marketing blitz can hold a candle to it. Nothing else on the planet compares to it in terms of the number of people celebrating it, the economic impact it has, and the amount of time we spend preparing for it, marking it, and recovering from it. No other holiday demands as much from us or gives us as much expectation, joy, and aggravation.

Christmas is kept by families all around the world and in many surprising ways. North Americans are familiar with it as a winter festival; we associate it with horse-drawn sleighs, snowflakes and snowmen, chestnuts roasting on an open fire, and Jack Frost nipping at our noses. But for many people Christmas arrives in the middle of summer and is associated with a barbecue and a day spent at the beach. We expect to see turkey and mashed potatoes on the table, but for others it wouldn't be Christmas without the traditional carp, or tamales, or rice porridge. We are not surprised to find carolers singing outside our doors, but how would we react to a procession of Star Boys, a parade for *las posadas*, or an *asalto* of visitors expecting rum? Our children look forward to the visit of Santa Claus, but kids and families around the world might anticipate the arrival of St. Nicholas, the Baby Jesus, the

Befana, Tante Arie, or the Three Kings. Gifts might magically appear on December 6, Christmas Eve, Christmas Day, New Year's Eve, or Epiphany, and the gift bringer might come pulled by reindeer, or alligators, or kangaroos; he might walk, she might ride a mule, or he might glide in on a surfboard.

Just as interesting as the myriad ways we keep Christmas today are the wonderful traditions of the past. The holiday has been celebrated for over seventeen hundred years, a period that stretches from the last days of the Roman Empire to the modern era. Christmas begins in the classical world, where gods such as Jupiter and Mars filled the public imagination and where holidays like Saturnalia, the Feast of the Unconquered Sun, and the Kalends entertained the pagan masses and even influenced how the Nativity of Christ was beginning to be celebrated. Then came the Dark Ages, when northern barbarians rampaged through the Roman Empire and had to be tamed by those whose lands they invaded and who kept Christmas. Again, a blend of new customs and old merged in the midwinter period; human and animal sacrifices gave way to Yule logs and a twelve-day rest from labor. As the empire crumbled, new nations and new languages emerged, new songs were sung, and new ceremonies were devised. Kings and emperors now wanted to be crowned or baptized at Christmas; feudal warfare was suspended during Christmas truces. During the Renaissance, princes commissioned the greatest artists to paint scenes of the Nativity or the journey of the Magi, while folk artisans carved miniature figures for crèches in churches and homes. The Industrial Revolution and its countless inventions, such as the railway, new materials, and chromolithography, created the opportunity for new Christmas practices like being able to come home for the holidays, putting up artificial trees, and sending Christmas cards.

FOREWORD

Christmas has seen many strange and wonderful customs come and go: witches (good and bad) and werewolves; shotguns and cannons; kisses and curses; unwanted guests and welcome strangers; girls seeking husbands by watching logs burn; races between flocks of turkey and geese; talking to livestock and beating up fruit trees. Is it good luck to be born on Christmas or bad? Will such a child be able to talk to the fairies or become a lawyer or a thief? What's a boy bishop? What's a wassail wench? Why is that man bringing a sheep into the church? Why shouldn't you ever set sail on December 28? Of the marvelous traditions of Yuletide, there is no end.

And who better to tell you these stories than Brian Earl, Christmas storyteller extraordinaire? Since 2016 he has been introducing listeners to the many wonders of the holiday, past and present. His enormously popular podcast *Christmas Past* is full of the history of the world's favorite festival, and now, with this book you hold in your hand, he is ready to make you even better informed and more in love with the season. What do you know about skeklers? Not much, I would think. How about Grandfather Frost or the Bean King? What about cross-dressing and Christmas? Is there a correct time to take down your seasonal decorations? Should you really engage in witty banter with those people carrying a horse's skull? The answers to these and a host of other Christmas mysteries lie within your grasp.

No matter what time of year it is now, find a comfy chair, sip a creamy eggnog, lean back, and read a chapter in *Of Christmases Long, Long Ago*.

Gerry Bowler, PhD
Author of *The World Encyclopedia of Christmas*,
Christmas in the Crosshairs, and more

Introduction

The months of September and October bring a change of season—the days grow shorter, the temperatures colder. Throughout most of history, this time of year also marked a dramatic change in lifestyle. The harvest was nearing completion; livestock herds would soon be thinned out. As winter loomed, it was a time to enjoy the literal and figurative fruits of the year's labor and strengthen social and familial ties.

And speaking of family and lifestyle changes, for many centuries in the Middle Ages, September and October also brought with them a noticeable increase in the birthrate. Some quick math tells us that the corresponding increase in the *conception* rate must have occurred right around Christmastime the previous year. Yes, Christmas may be the jolliest time of the year, but our ancestors interpreted that sentiment quite differently than we do today—and not just when it came to contributing to the birthrate. In many ways, the Christmases of long, long ago were a hot, merry mess of drinking, fornicating, and gambling— and that's just for starters.

The Puritan clergyman (and former Harvard president) Increase Mather wrote in 1687 that all the hedonism and debauchery associated with Christmas had earned the season the nickname *Mensis Genialis*, or the "Voluptuous Month." Fellow Puritan Phillip Stubbes was writing about this idea more than a century before. In his 1583 book *The Anatomie of Abuses*, Stubbes decries how, during Christmas, "more mischief is that time committed than in all the year besides. What masking and mumming! Whereby robbery, whoredom, murder, and what not is committed!"

Robbery. Whoredom. Murder. Merry Christmas!

On the one hand, it's easy enough to imagine that Christmas in the distant past must have been very different from today. Twinkling lights, Santa Claus, Christmas movies, Bing Crosby's music, wrapped gifts—these are all creations of the last 150 years or so. Christmases throughout the vast majority of history didn't include any of them. On the other hand, it's not so easy for us to imagine exactly *how* it was different. The differences include not just the modern creations it lacked but also how and when it was celebrated.

Our current version of Christmas is a product of the nineteenth century, fueled by a rising middle class, booming industrialism, and myriad advances in technology and infrastructure. This "domesticated" version of Christmas is a rather innocent, cozy family affair, filled with gifts, children's characters, and decorated cookies. It is a mixture of the sacred and the secular, with the secular constantly expanding its share.

It's only natural to assume that before all that, Christmas must have been a much more solemn observance. After all, people were more devoutly religious in previous eras untarnished by the luxuries and distractions of the modern world. But boy, would you be wrong! Instead, Christmas was a wild spree in which Christians would cast off their usual moral restraints to overindulge and misbehave in ways large and small.

PHILLIP STUBBES'S ANATOMY

OF THE

ABUSES IN ENGLAND

IN

SHAKSPERE'S YOUTH,

A.D. 1583.

PART I.

Title page for an 1877 edition of Phillip Stubbes's 1583 book, originally published as *The Anatomie of Abuses*. SOURCE: INTERNET ARCHIVE.

This carnival-style celebration wasn't unique to Christmas. In fact, Christmas very clearly continued these ideas from earlier festivals like Dies Natalis Solis Invicti (Birthday of the Invincible Sun), Kalends, Saturnalia, and Yuletide. And it did so for the same reasons as its predecessors. Sanctioning a period of "letting loose" and upending the normal social order made it easier to maintain that social order the rest of the time.

As we'll see in many of the traditions explored in this book, "social inversion," role reversal, and free speech were big themes. Men dressed like women and vice versa, boys dressed like bishops, and many people dressed as animals. People got wasted, got loud, danced up a storm, and stuffed their faces.

For the rowdy revelers of the past, Christmas arrived at the end of the monthlong fast of Advent. Anyone hoping that Christmas past was a time of piousness and devotion can at least take solace in knowing that Advent fits that description. By Christmas Day, all that self-restraint had reached its breaking point. The floodgates would then open to a glorious twelve days of excess and playful misrule.

That twelve-day period is one of the key differences between Christmas then and now. Today, the "Christmas season" is the period leading *up to* Christmas Day. Here in America, that period begins just after Thanksgiving and lasts for around a month, ending with Christmas Day itself. But, as just mentioned, that same period was traditionally already spoken for by the observance of Advent. So, for most of Christmas history, the season *began* with Christmas instead of ending with it.

All that letting loose at the end of Advent got started in the sixth century—and by church decree, no less. Since the year 336, Christmas

INTRODUCTION

has been observed on December 25. In 563, the Council of Braga forbade fasting on Christmas Day. And a short four years later, in 567, the Council of Tours established the twelve days of Christmas, a period of feasting and celebration that began on Christmas Day and ended with Twelfth Night (Epiphany Eve).

So, in this book, you'll learn about many "Christmas traditions" that were observed, for example, on New Year's Day or January 5. This arrangement may sound odd to modern celebrants, but that's the way it was throughout most of history. Only in the past two centuries have the twelve days of Christmas largely faded.

Surely, the Councils of Braga and Tours didn't foresee all the ways that the twelve days of Christmas would go off the rails. By the Middle Ages, it was "the twelve days of Christmas meets the seven deadly sins." Clergy, commonfolk, and aristocracy alike all had their own brands of misrule, as you're about to discover. Over time, all kinds of cultural beliefs and folk traditions also worked their way into Christmas. As we'll see, Christmas past was filled with ghosts, monsters, concealed identities, ritual animal disguise, gunfire, riots, and lots of alcohol. We'll meet cross-dressing priests, drunken beggars, child-abusing gift bringers, and elected mischief makers.

Of course it wasn't all about gluttony, carousing, and upsetting the social order (even if those are the most fun to talk about). We'll also encounter beliefs about bringing good luck to the home, systems for saving money and giving charity, fortune-telling, and a handful of colorful anecdotes and pieces of classic literature. We'll travel through the Middle Ages into the nineteenth and early twentieth centuries. And while many of the traditions we'll discover are truly relics of the past, a select few do carry on (to varying degrees) in the present day.

I've divided the book into seven parts: "Social Inversion," "Parties and Feasts," "Raucous Revels," "Money and Charity," "Keeping House," "Gift Bringers," and "The Wild Side." Naturally, there will be overlap among these sections. Some of the traditions we'll encounter could be examples of both social inversion and feasting, for example. But the parts are meant not just to place these traditions into exclusive categories but also to call out many of the dominant themes of Christmas in olden times.

As we get ready to dive into the surprising traditions and stories from Christmas past, I'll leave you with this handy glossary of terms, as they've traditionally related to the twelve days of Christmas and the Western calendar. This will save you the trouble of having the same information repeated throughout the chapters that follow.

Advent (Moveable): The period starting on the fourth Sunday before Christmas and ending with Christmas Eve.

Childermas (December 28): Also known as the Feast of the Holy Innocents, commemorates the biblical story of King Herod ordering the slaughter of all male children under age two near Bethlehem.

Christmas Eve (December 24): The vigil before Christmas and the final day of Advent.

Christmas Day (December 25): The celebration observing the birth of Jesus and the beginning of the twelve days of Christmas.

Epiphany (January 6): Also known as the Feast of the Epiphany or Three Kings Day, a celebration commemorating the visit of the Magi to the baby Jesus.

INTRODUCTION

Epiphany Eve (January 5): Also known as Twelfth Night, the close of the Christmas season.

New Year's Day (January 1): The first day of the year; also known as the Feast of the Naming and Circumcision of Jesus and the Solemnity of Mary, Mother of God.

New Year's Eve (December 31): The final day of the year.

Saint Stephen's Day (December 26): The day commemorating the first Christian martyr; also known as the Feast of Stephen and Gŵyl San Steffan (in Wales). In addition, December 26 is Boxing Day, which is often conflated with Saint Stephen's Day, though they are distinct observances.

Twelfth Night (January 5): See Epiphany Eve.

Twelve Days of Christmas (December 25–January 5): Also called Christmastide, Christ-tide, and Twelvetide, the period of twelve days of festivities following Advent.

Illustration of a Christmas masquerade, 1837. SOURCE: WIKIPEDIA.

PART 1
Social Inversion

Down is up, wrong is right, and Christmas bells are ringing. In the Christmases of centuries ago, ethical norms were abandoned, and the social hierarchy was turned upside down. During Christmas revels, people had temporary license to dress, behave, and consume in ways that would be unthinkable at any other time of year. Drinking, gambling, cross-dressing, and overindulging of all kinds ruled the day. Let's dive into the topsy-turvy world of Christmas past.

SOURCE: DOROTHY SIEMENS.

CHAPTER 1
Cross-Dressing
Christmas in Drag

The Isles of Scilly (pronounced "silly") are an archipelago off the southwestern tip of Cornwall, England. And silly indeed was a Christmas custom practiced there, described in John Troutbeck's 1796 *A Survey of the Ancient and Present State of the Scilly Islands*:

> At Christmastime, the young people exercise a sort of gallantry among them, which they call goose dancing, when the maidens are dressed up for young men, and the young men for maidens. . . . The maidens who are sometimes dressed up for sea captains and other officers, display their alluring graces to the ladies, who are young men equipped for the purpose; and the ladies exert their talents to them in courtley address.

Christmas cross-dressing is an example of the merry misrule and role reversal of Christmases long, long ago. It belongs to the larger concept of "masking," the use of costumes and disguises as part of a celebration, often as part of some kind of performance (see MASKING).

It was common on Twelfth Night and occasions throughout the twelve days of Christmas.

Cross-dressing wasn't limited to gender swapping. Members of the clergy would also don the clothes of members of higher or lower status in the church hierarchy, for instance (see THE BOY BISHOP). Or common folk would sometimes dress as royalty.

As for so many other examples of social inversion, we can thank the ancient Romans for this custom. During the wintertime feast of Saturnalia, cross-dressing of all kinds was part of the debauched jollity of it all.

But just because it became common at Christmastime, that doesn't mean everybody was happy about it. In the fifteenth century, the theology faculty at the University of Paris issued a joint letter denouncing the Christmastime celebration of the Feast of Fools. In their letter, they made a special point of calling out cross-dressing among priests and clerks (see THE FEAST OF FOOLS).

Christmastime cross-dressing is mostly extinct now. However, some faint echoes of Christmas past remain. In England, pantomimes dominate the theatrical calendar during the Christmas season. This style of theater prominently features cross-dressed characters. And Christmas-themed drag performances have become part of the holiday landscape in many American cities.

CROSS-DRESSING

SATURNALIA

The Bacchanal That Started It All?

Illustration showing Saturnalia being celebrated, 1884. SOURCE: NEW YORK PUBLIC LIBRARY.

The Roman Saturnalia was hugely influential on early Christmas celebrations. Here are some interesting facts about this delightfully debauched ancient holiday.

> *It honored the god Saturn.* In Roman myth, Saturn was an agricultural god. A huge public banquet was held at the Temple of Saturn for Saturnalia.
>
> *It was a time for topsy-turvy role reversal.* Saturnalia was a time for a drastic change of attitude and behavior. During the festival, people were freed from normal social rules and restraints. Slaves

were treated to a banquet, people cross-dressed, free speech pervaded, and little was taken seriously.

It was crazy dress-up day. The aristocracy ditched their traditional conservative togas in favor of brightly colored clothes. This style of dress, known as "synthesis" (meaning "to be put together"), would have been considered in poor taste at any other time. People would also wear a brimless, cone-shaped hat usually worn by slaves who had been awarded their freedom. The idea was that *everyone* was free during Saturnalia.

They indulged in games of chance. During Saturnalia, activities like gambling and dice playing, typically forbidden or frowned on, were allowed for everyone, including slaves.

All of Rome shut down. All forms of work—even exercise—stopped during the celebration. Schools, businesses, and courts were closed, and it was against the rules to declare war during the celebration.

There was a master of revels. A drawing was held to elect a "ruler of Saturnalia" to serve as master of ceremonies. In addition to leading the revels, this "ruler" could give out silly, capricious commands, which people were expected to obey.

It was a minor gift-giving holiday. Gifts were exchanged, but only in a manner in keeping with Saturnalia's theme of bucking the social hierarchy. Valuable gifts would convey social status, so they were a no-no. Instead, pottery, candles, figurines, and various gag gifts were common.

Revelers were acting out a myth. The revelries were meant to reflect or restore the state of things from the mythical "golden age" when Saturn ruled the world.

CROSS-DRESSING

Modern historians had to piece it all together. You'd think that, as it was the best-known Roman holiday, at least one ancient writer would have produced an account of it. But no, they must have been too busy drinking with the rest of Rome. Our understanding was pulled together from several texts that mention different parts of it.

It remained popular, even after Christianity took over. People celebrated Saturnalia for nearly four hundred years after the Roman Empire came under Christian dominion. During that period, many of its customs carried over into Christmas celebrations.

It must have been a great time, because they kept extending it. The festival was originally held on December 17. Later, it was extended to three days, December 17–19. Finally it was extended to seven days, December 17–23.

It wasn't the only game in town. Saturnalia was one of many celebrations like it in the Greco-Roman world. Its Greek equivalent is the holiday known as Kronia. Other similar celebrations honoring different gods are known to have existed in regions of Greece and Babylon.

There was a traditional greeting. Just like we wish one another a "merry Christmas," so, too, did the ancient Romans have their own way of spreading holiday cheer. The traditional salutation was "io Saturnalia!"

SOURCE: DOROTHY SIEMENS.

CHAPTER 2
The Boy Bishop
Out of the Mouths of Babes

Timing is everything, they say. And Christmas as we know it might have looked a lot different had it not been for the fortunate timing of one Nicholas of Myra, the man who became Saint Nicholas. But before he was a saint, he was a priest and then a bishop. And how did he get that promotion? True story: The bishop in the city of Myra, where Nicholas lived, had recently died. The priests of Myra came up with a surprising strategy to consecrate a successor. The plan was that the first priest to enter the church that morning would get the job. And that priest just happened to be Nicholas.

And that's not even the most surprising thing about the story. The real kicker was that Nicholas was only thirty years old at the time, which was almost unheard of. The age of thirty was practically boyhood compared to the age of most bishops.

Nicholas's appearance in the right place at the right time did two important things: First, it set the course for the rest of his life, which in turn formed the basis for a big part of how Christmas would later be celebrated. And second, it may have gotten people reconsidering their beliefs about the appropriate age for bishops.

Fast-forward to the Middle Ages, when churches had a custom of choosing a choirboy to impersonate a bishop as part of certain church celebrations. In his role, the "boy bishop" would dress in a bishop's robes, lead church services, appoint some of his friends as mock chaplains, and give blessings.

At first, the idea was that by letting the youngsters experience a bit of officiating, they might consider a life in the priesthood. But that all changed when the boy bishop became part of Childermas (also known as the Feast of the Holy Innocents) during the twelve days of Christmas. At that point, the custom became less solemn and more an example of the topsy-turvy social inversion and misrule of Christmas past. As a result, churches restricted the custom to Saint Nicholas Day on December 6. Now that it was outside the twelve days of Christmas, the thinking went, the honor and dignity of the role would be restored.

But that's not what happened. The misrule continued to . . . well, rule. And so the custom was eventually suppressed. King Henry VIII banned it in 1541. Over the following centuries, the boy bishop tradition made a few brief comebacks, but by the seventeenth century, it was gone for good.

A REAL CHARACTER
The Boy Bishop Takes the Stage

Mystère de la Nativité du Christ is a thirteenth-century play that introduced the character of Episcopus Puerorum ("bishop of the boys"). In his 1907 book *Plays of Our Forefathers, and Some of the Traditions on Which They Were Founded*, Charles Gayley writes,

THE BOY BISHOP

In this mystery the Episcopus Puerorum plays, indeed, no extended part: he rebukes the High Priest and the Jews for their unbelief in the miraculous birth, and refers the prophets to St. Augustine for verification of their predictions; but the manner of his dramatic appearance points to the religious quality of his origin. His character was familiar to the church from remote times.

In fact, King Conrad I was known to have witnessed a procession featuring a boy bishop in the year 911 at the monastery at Saint Gall, where he was impressed by the children's discipline. Gayley cites this historical account:

It would be a long story to tell what pleasures he had by day and night, especially in the procession of the children; and he was amazed at their discipline, for though he had ordered that apples should be strewn before them down the middle of the aisle, not even the tiniest lad broke ranks or stretched his hand out to get one.

A Monument to a Boy-Bishop
From "Ancient Mysteries Described"

Illustration of Episcopus Puerorum from Charles Gayley's *Plays of Our Forefathers, and Some of the Traditions on Which They Were Founded*.
SOURCE: INTERNET ARCHIVE.

SOURCE: DOROTHY SIEMENS.

CHAPTER 3
The Feast of Fools
A Pie in the Face of Piety

The ancient Romans sure knew how to party. Gluttony, drunkenness, and carousing—just another day in the life of a feasting Roman. At year's end, three wild winter wingdings followed one after the other. First was the weeklong Saturnalia in mid-December, honoring Saturn, the god of agriculture. Up next was Dies Natalis Solis Invicti (Birthday of the Invincible Sun), held at the solstice in honor of Sol Invictus, the sun god. And capping it off in early January was a celebration that didn't involve any ancient gods. In fact, at face value, it sounds like some sort of boring administrative holiday.

The celebration was called Kalends, and it marked the beginning of the legislative year, when new consuls took office. But don't be fooled. Kalends was every bit as drunk and disorderly as any feast worthy of ancient Rome.

Technically, the beginning of every month was known as Kalends, but the one in January was the big one. The celebration officially went from January 1 to January 3, but unofficially it often extended further.

"The Festival of Fools" engraving, 1570. SOURCE: WIKIMEDIA COMMONS.

There was a strong current of role reversal. Masters waited on their servants. Senators dressed as plebeians. Men dressed as women.

Kalends is recognized as the predecessor to the Feast of Fools. In the Middle Ages, starting on January 1, low-ranking clergy chose a "Bishop of Fools" (alternatively, a "Fools' Pope") to lead a period of impious merrymaking. Gambling, gluttony, cross-dressing, practical jokes: that's just the warm-up. Running in church, using the soles of old shoes for incense—this was hardly the stuff of solemn subdeacons in daily life. But it most certainly was the stuff of the Feast of Fools.

Later, the Feast of Fools was celebrated by clergy and laity alike. When things started getting out of hand (as they were bound to do), both the church and the monarchy tried to ban the Feast of Fools. Even so, it carried on for centuries before finally fading away.

THE FEAST OF FOOLS

QUASIMODO, POPE OF THE FOOLS
The Hunchback of Christmas Past

The Feast of Fools is featured in a work of classic literature. In Victor Hugo's 1831 novel *The Hunchback of Notre-Dame*, the title character is elected Pope of the Fools on Twelfth Night. The scene, set in 1482 and excerpted below, depicts a period in which the Feast of Fools was observed by both clergy and nonclergy.

> The Pope of the Fools had been elected.
> "Noël! Noël! Noël!" shouted the people on all sides. That was, in fact, a marvellous grimace which was beaming at that moment through the aperture in the rose window. After all the pentagonal, hexagonal, and whimsical faces, which had succeeded each other at that hole without realizing the ideal of the grotesque which their imaginations, excited by the orgy, had constructed, nothing less was needed to win their suffrages than the sublime grimace which had just dazzled the assembly. Master Coppenole himself applauded, and Clopin Trouillefou, who had been among the competitors (and God knows what intensity of ugliness his visage could attain), confessed himself conquered: We will do the same. We shall not try to give the reader an idea of that tetrahedral nose, that horseshoe mouth; that little left eye obstructed with a red, bushy, bristling eyebrow, while the right eye disappeared entirely beneath an enormous wart; of those teeth in disarray, broken here and there, like the

embattled parapet of a fortress; of that callous lip, upon which one of these teeth encroached, like the tusk of an elephant; of that forked chin; and above all, of the expression spread over the whole; of that mixture of malice, amazement, and sadness. Let the reader dream of this whole, if he can.

The acclamation was unanimous; people rushed towards the chapel. They made the lucky Pope of the Fools come forth in triumph. But it was then that surprise and admiration attained their highest pitch; the grimace was his face.

Or rather, his whole person was a grimace. A huge head, bristling with red hair; between his shoulders an enormous hump, a counterpart perceptible in front; a system of thighs and legs so strangely astray that they could touch each other only at the knees, and, viewed from the front, resembled the crescents of two scythes joined by the handles; large feet, monstrous hands; and, with all this deformity, an indescribable and redoubtable air of vigor, agility, and courage,—strange exception to the eternal rule which wills that force as well as beauty shall be the result of harmony. Such was the pope whom the fools had just chosen for themselves.

One would have pronounced him a giant who had been broken and badly put together again.

When this species of cyclops appeared on the threshold of the chapel, motionless, squat, and almost as broad as he was tall; *squared* on the *base*, as a great man says; with his doublet half red, half violet, sown with silver bells, and, above all, in the perfection of his ugliness, the populace recognized him on the instant, and shouted with one voice,—

THE FEAST OF FOOLS

"'Tis Quasimodo, the bellringer! 'tis Quasimodo, the hunchback of Notre-Dame! Quasimodo, the one-eyed! Quasimodo, the bandy-legged! Noël! Noël!"

. . .

In the meantime, all the beggars, all the lackeys, all the cutpurses, joined with the scholars, had gone in procession to seek, in the cupboard of the law clerks' company, the cardboard tiara, and the derisive robe of the Pope of the Fools. Quasimodo allowed them to array him in them without wincing, and with a sort of proud docility. Then they made him seat himself on a motley litter. Twelve officers of the fraternity of fools raised him on their shoulders; and a sort of bitter and disdainful joy lighted up the morose face of the cyclops, when he beheld beneath his deformed feet all those heads of handsome, straight, well-made men. Then the ragged and howling procession set out on its march, according to custom, around the inner galleries of the Courts, before making the circuit of the streets and squares.

Charles Laughton as the Hunchback of Notre Dame from the eponymous film of 1939. SOURCE: PHOTOFEST.

SOURCE: DOROTHY SIEMENS.

CHAPTER 4
The Bean King
Of Luck and Legumes

The twelfth day of Christmas may have been the day when someone's true love sent twelve drummers drumming. But if you celebrated Christmas long, long ago, it may also have been the day of another Christmas surprise: being crowned "the Bean King" and made the leader of Christmas festivities.

Twelfth Night was the last hurrah before the Christmas season came to an end. And what better way to bid Christmas a festive farewell than with one last raucous feast?

The custom of electing a "king" of the festivities is yet another example of Christmastime social inversion and mock authority figures (see THE BOY BISHOP and THE LORD OF MISRULE). The means of electing a "king" by hiding a bean in a special "Twelfth cake" or "Twelfth Night cake" may have originated in the thirteenth century. The custom was especially popular in France, where the festive cake was known as the *gâteau des rois*, or "King's Cake." There are records of it from as early as the reign of Edward II. One sixteenth-century account of the custom describes how it worked:

> When the cake has been cut into as many portions as there are guests, a small child is put under the table. . . . Thereupon the master calls on him to say to whom he shall give the piece of cake which he has in his hand; the child names whoever comes into his head. . . . He who gets it is reckoned king of the company. . . . This done, everyone eats, drinks, and dances heartily.

There were variations on the selection process, but the basic idea was always the same. A "queen" was often also appointed. The Bean King presided over the rest of the evening's activities, sometimes giving playful commands to his "subjects." The king's "reign" ended at midnight, when the Christmas season officially ended and the world returned to normal. The Bean King custom had largely fizzled out by the nineteenth century.

BAKE YOUR OWN BEAN KING CAKE
Bean Not Included

Want to party like it's 1599 and crown a Bean King of your own? To bring a bit of Christmas past into your festivities, all you need is a dry bean, a Christmas cake recipe, and a fun-loving cast of friends and family to join the revels.

As far as the bean and the family and friends go, you're on your own. But for the cake recipe, Isabella Beeton is here to help. Known simply as "Mrs. Beeton" to generations of householders, her 1861

The Book of Household Management is a one-thousand-plus-page compendium of instructions for all areas of managing a home. Naturally, a large portion of the book is dedicated to cooking and baking, including seasonal fare.

This recipe for a Christmas cake is a good example of the kinds of Christmas cakes served for centuries: a dense, rich, spiced cake, studded with dried fruit. Just don't forget to stir a dry bean into the batter!

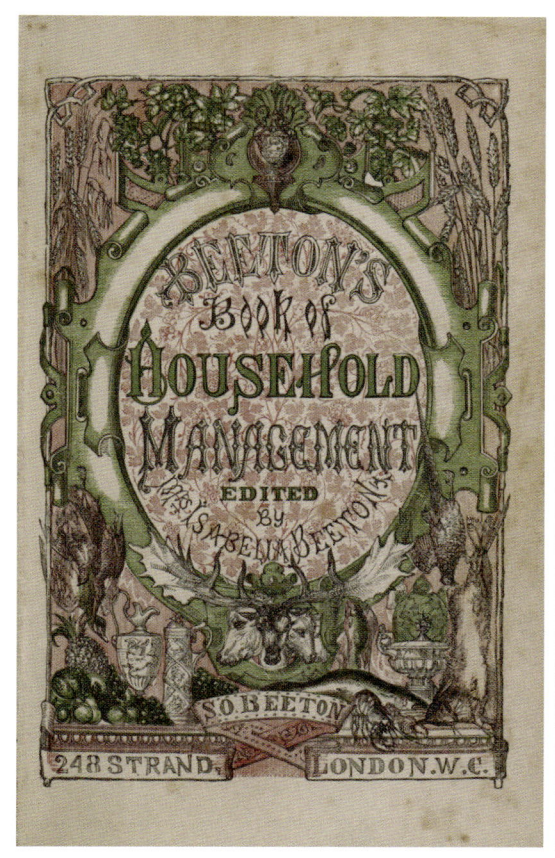

Title page for Mrs. Beeton's *The Book of Household Management.* SOURCE: LIBRARY OF CONGRESS.

Mrs. Beeton's recipe for a traditional Christmas cake. SOURCE: LIBRARY OF CONGRESS.

BRINGING IN THE BOAR'S HEAD.

Illustration of a boar's head procession, *New York Tribune*, 1907. SOURCE: LIBRARY OF CONGRESS.

PART 2
Parties and Feasts

Present-day Christmas parties tend to be cozy and well behaved compared to those of long ago. Sure, we have our own brand of revelry off the rails, typically in the form of ugly sweater parties and a few too many spiked eggnogs. But that's nothing compared to the sanctioned misrule, concealed identities, dangerous games, weird foods, and drunken carrying on of Christmas past.

As we dive into the Christmas parties and feasts of centuries ago, once again we'll see the idea of social inversion woven throughout the twelve days . . . and a little dash of danger for good measure!

SOURCE: DOROTHY SIEMENS.

CHAPTER 5
The Lord of Misrule
Master of Merry Disports

Christmastime is a season with a stacked cast of characters: a right jolly old elf; a red-nosed reindeer; a miserly Scrooge; a snowman with a happy, jolly soul; and the list goes on.

Notably absent from the list: a mischievous court-jester-like figure who encourages you to engage in bawdy, drunken revels. But he wasn't always absent. In late medieval and early Tudor England, a "Lord of Misrule" was specially appointed in royal courts and the households of noblemen to lead Christmas festivities. Law schools and other colleges at the universities of Cambridge and Oxford also appointed their own Lords of Misrule.

The position was typically assigned to a peasant or low-ranking member of the clergy, who was to serve, as one historian described it, as a "master of merry disports." The position lasted through the twelve days of Christmas (and often beyond). During this time, the Lord of Misrule acted as a master of ceremonies, arranging and presiding over entertainment, games, and feasts. These festivities often included costume parties, plays, and parades. It was a coveted position, and those appointed to it took the job very seriously.

It wasn't uncommon for nobles to bring their own Lords of Misrule along with them when attending Christmas revels, thereby multiplying the festive folly! As one sixteenth-century historian recounts, "The mayor of London, and either of the sheriffs, had their several lords of misrule, ever contending, without quarrel or offence, who should make the rarest pastimes to delight the beholders."

The idea of a Lord of Misrule is likely borrowed from the "Ruler of Saturnalia" custom from the Roman Saturnalia celebration (see SATURNALIA). While it is mostly an English tradition, Scotland had its own version: the "Abbot of Unreason."

But, like the Lord of Misrule's reign during the twelve days of Christmas, all good things must come to an end. Eventually, when the practice was deemed too disruptive, it was discouraged and ultimately banned.

"Twelfth Night (The King Drinks)," by David Teniers the Younger, circa 1650. SOURCE: WIKIPEDIA.

OF LORDS AND LADIES
The Lord of Misrule Gets Married!

The Lord of Misrule typically acted alone, leading the riotous revels with a singular blend of mirth and whimsy. However, it's not without precedent that the "lord" should be accompanied by a "lady." And it's certainly not without precedent that a license for misrule often led to things getting out of hand.

In his 1894 book *A Righte Merrie Christmas!! The Story of Christ-tide*, John Ashton reports this curious case from Christmas past:

> The Commissioners for Causes Ecclesiastical kept strict watch on some of the Christmas revellers of 1637. They had before them one Saunders, from Lincolnshire, for carrying revelry too far. Saunders and others, at Blatherwick, had appointed a Lord of Misrule over their festivities. This was perfectly lawful, and could not be gainsaid. But they had resolved that he should have a lady, or Christmas wife; and probably there would have been no harm in that, if they had not carried the matter too far. They, however, brought in as bride one Elizabeth Pitto, daughter of the hog-herd of the town. Saunders received her, disguised as a parson, wearing a shirt or smock for a surplice. He then married the Lord of Misrule to the hog-herd's daughter, reading the whole of the marriage service from the Book of Common Prayer. All the after ceremonies and customs then in use were observed, and the affair was carried to its utmost extent. The parties had time to repent at leisure in prison.

SOURCE: DOROTHY SIEMENS.

CHAPTER 6

Masking

Christmas in Disguise

Don we now our gay . . . disguises? Christmas may be a time for festively fabulous party wear, but masks and costumes probably don't come to mind these days. If you traveled in royal circles centuries ago, though, your Christmas revels probably looked a lot like a modern-day Halloween party. As far back as the 1300s, the custom of wearing disguises to Christmas celebrations seems to have taken hold. King Charles VI of France was known to host Christmas masquerade parties, one of which involved a notable tragedy. In 1393, several partygoers wore costumes that included flammable substances. When they got too close to some flaming torches, their costumes caught fire. Several people died, and King Charles himself was said to have barely escaped the ordeal in one piece.

Stating the obvious, drunken revels and concealed identities are a perfect recipe for danger and disorder of all kinds. Even though King Henry VIII of England was a "lustie" (old-time speak for "enthusiastic") masker, he saw fit to pass a law against it after a few parties got out of hand on his watch.

Masking (or "guising," as it was also sometimes known) wasn't limited to upper-crust parties. Various other traditions combined Christmas and disguises (see THE MARI LWYD, SKEKLERS, and THE BROAD). "Mumming" is a special kind of Christmas performance done in disguise. Mummer's plays have declined in popularity over time, but you can still find some performances today in England, Ireland, Scotland, and the Isle of Man. Philadelphia also hosts an annual Mummer's Day Parade on New Year's Day.

CHRISTMAS, HIS MASQUE
Christmas Is a Dad

Sometimes there's a fine line between mummer's plays (which are more of a folk custom) and masques (festive plays performed in costume in royal courts). Ben Jonson's *Christmas, His Masque* debuted in the royal court of King James I in 1616.

Though many critics wrote it off as a mere mummer's play, it artfully addressed some weighty topics. By 1616, the Puritans were already taking aim at Christmas as "popish." Jonson's main character, a personification of Christmas, throws barbs at the Puritans:

> I have seen the time you have wish'd for me for a merry Christmas; and now you have me, they would not let me in: I must come another time! a good jest, as if I could come more than once a year! Why, I am no dangerous person, and so I told my friends of the guard. I am old Gregory Christmas still, and though I come out of Pope's-head alley, as good a Protestant as any in my parish.

MASKING

In the masque, Christmas's ten children—Misrule, Carol, Minced-Pie, Gambol, Post and Pair, New-Year's-Gift, Mumming, Wassel, Offering, and Baby-Cake—are led on stage by Cupid, and they sing,

Now God preserve, as you do well deserve,
Your majesties all, two there;
Your highness small, with my good lords all,
And ladies, how do you do there?

Give me leave to ask, for I bring you a masque
From little, little, little London;
Which say the king likes, I have passed the pikes,
If not, old Christmas is undone.

Illustration from *The Book of Christmas* by Thomas Kibble Hervey, 1836.
SOURCE: WIKIMEDIA COMMONS.

SOURCE: DOROTHY SIEMENS.

CHAPTER 7
Dangerous Games
Christmas Eve: Contact Sport

Bumps. Bruises. First-degree burns. Why, it must be Christmas Eve!

The Victorians loved their parlor games. But it wasn't always well-mannered games of charades played out in stately drawing rooms. The Victorians were actually pioneers of perilous partying! Come Christmas Eve, some parlor games were a chance not only to make the season bright but also to stare danger in the eye.

Combine the jollity of the season, the relaxation of social norms, and freely flowing alcohol, and you have the makings of festive folly that you'd be lucky to escape in one piece.

One example was the game of Snapdragon. On a table in a dimly lit parlor sits a wide, shallow bowl filled with raisins floating in brandy. The brandy is set alight, sending blue flames flickering. One by one, the players attempt the fiery feat of quickly reaching into the bowl, plucking out a raisin, and popping it into their mouth.

If the idea of scorched skin doesn't have you feeling festive, perhaps getting whacked upside the head is your preferred brand of merry

Illustration of a game of blind man's bluff from *Ballou's Pictorial Drawing-Room Companion*, 1857. SOURCE: BOSTON PUBLIC LIBRARY.

mayhem. In that case, Hot Cockles is the game for you. In it, a blindfolded person kneels down, gets a whack on the head, and then has to guess who hit him. Yes, that's literally the whole game. And yes, we assume that the person getting hit was always a *him*.

Or perhaps you'd like to take the derring-do up another notch. Then why not try a game of blind man's bluff? But not today's watered-down version of the game, in which a blindfolded player simply gropes around trying to tag the other players. No, in Victorian times, blind man's bluff was much more violent at Christmastime. Blindfolded players risked bumps and bruises as they careened into obstacles strategically placed in their way by mischievous hosts. An observer once quipped that this version of the game must have been dreamed up by "country bone setters" as a means of attracting business.

DANGEROUS GAMES

GAMBLING
Merrily We Roll the Dice

Gambling was common throughout the Middle Ages, even though it was condemned by the church and even outlawed in many places. But in the spirit of merry misrule for Christmastime, church and state alike made an exception. In the fifteenth century, for example, King Henry VIII forbade gambling among servants and apprentices throughout England, *except* during Christmas.

Everybody took part: young and old, male and female, clergy and laity, aristocracy and common folk. It wasn't even unheard of to play games of chance right on the church altar! Gambling was as common a Christmas tradition as feasting and singing.

One of the most popular gambling games of the age was a dice game called Hazard. Playing cards, though common in China since the ninth century, wouldn't reach Europe until the fourteenth century. When they did, they quickly became a favorite for gambling games of all kinds.

An uncut sheet of playing cards by French designer André Perrocet, circa 1500. SOURCE: WIKIMEDIA COMMONS.

SOURCE: DOROTHY SIEMENS.

CHAPTER 8
Gross Foods
A Gastronomic Gag Fest

Just a few generations ago, Christmas was a season featuring some head-scratching culinary creations. Magazines and cookbooks of the 1960s and 1970s featured pâté-cheese balls set in a gelatin mold, tuna shaped into a Christmas tree, and various other crimes against taste buds.

But if you think old Aunt Mary's "turkey surprise casserole" was bad, just wait 'til you hear about the gross foods of Christmas past.

Many a medieval Christmas banquet featured the severed head of a boar, often elaborately decorated with rosemary and an apple stuffed in its mouth, served on a platter. The presentation of the boar's head was often a celebration in itself, accompanied by the singing of "The Boar's Head Carol."

Haxey Hood was a game played on Twelfth Night in which the men of two villages would play for possession of a leather ball. However, according to one account, an actual boar's head was wrestled for one Christmas Day at Hornsuch in Essex. The winners then took it to the public house of their village for a Christmas feast.

The Boar's Head Carol.
SOURCE: LIBRARY OF CONGRESS.

If the sight of a severed head doesn't whet your appetite, perhaps you're more of a "stately pye" person. That was a peacock pie, common in the sixteenth century among those who could afford it. The pie was served with the peacock's head protruding from the crust, with its beak decorated. At the other end of the pie, the bird's tail feathers were spread out in full display.

If you don't care to see the physical form of the animal you're eating, then brawn may be the choice for you. All the rage during the time of Queen Elizabeth I, it was a jellied loaf or mold made from parts of an animal's head, feet, and sometimes tongue and heart. The latter-day equivalent of brawn is known as "head cheese." Part of the reason brawn became a Christmas favorite was that, in a quirky bit of classification, it was officially recognized as a kind of fish. That allowed Christians to indulge in it throughout the fasting days of Advent as well as the feasting during the twelve days of Christmas.

BRAWN WE NOW OUR CHRISTMAS DINNER

Have a Holly Jellied Christmas

Thinking of walking in your ancestors' culinary footsteps and boiling up a batch of brawn for the Christmas dinner table? The good news is that you have a choice between the calf's head and the pig's head varieties. The bad news is that, either way, you still end up with brawn.

Eliza Acton's 1887 cookbook *Modern Cookery for Private Families* offers up one way to make a calf's head brawn.

Calf's head brawn recipe from *Modern Cookery for Private Families*.
SOURCE: LIBRARY OF CONGRESS.

Revelers making raucous, noisy "music."
SOURCE: WIKIMEDIA COMMONS.

PART 3
Raucous Revels

Silent night, you say? All is calm, you say? Spoken like someone accustomed to Christmas in the twentieth and twenty-first centuries! Prior to that, Christmas was anything but *silent and calm. Raucous, unruly, noisy, often profane, and sometimes violent—the Christmases of long, long ago give new meaning to that Yuletide lyric "you better watch out."*

Let's travel back to a time when riots, gunfire, and practical jokes were common sights and sounds of the season.

SOURCE: DOROTHY SIEMENS.

CHAPTER 9
Callithumpian Parades
Things That Go Bump in the Night

New Year's Eve revelers are no strangers to the peals of novelty noise makers or the boom and crackle of fireworks. But if you lived in eighteenth-century England or New York, you might find yourself "treated" to an altogether different kind of noise, in the form of rowdy revelry carried out by a "callithumpian" band.

The word "callithumpian" possibly derives from the Greek *calli*, meaning "beautiful." But don't be fooled. Callithumpian bands were not made up of real musicians, and the sounds they made were anything but beautiful. They aimed to be boisterous and provocative, banging on pans (or anything that could make a racket), blaring horns and whistles, and yelling—all intended to annoy and ridicule.

Who were these "musicians"? Whom were they trying to ridicule and why? And why during the twelve days of Christmas?

Traditionally, the social-inversion element so common in Christmas celebrations of the past was controlled by authority figures, whether from the ruling class or the clergy. But that all began to change in the eighteenth century, when some people decided to take matters into their own hands. Their brand of social inversion was less about fun and games and "letting off steam" and more a form of protest. The callithumpian bands were one such form and aimed their noisy parades at those they deemed too rich and powerful.

Callithumpian parades belong to a folk custom known as "rough music." It has gone by many other names—charivary, loo-belling, and stang riding, among others—and was usually staged as a mock serenade, aimed at publicly shaming or punishing a member of the community. It was especially common to protest the weddings of old widowers to young women with a rough-music serenade.

The first reports of callithumpian parades come from England in the eighteenth century. By the early nineteenth century, the phenomenon had crossed the Atlantic, and New York had its own callithumpians. In one notable example from 1826, marauders descended on the neighborhoods that were home to New York City's rich and powerful. Things turned violent as the gang marched toward the city hall, stopping at taverns and a church along the way, where they smashed windows, broke down doors, and vandalized property.

CALLITHUMPIAN PARADES

ON THE POLICE BEAT

Shush . . . in the Name of the Law!

Once callithumpian parades had reached America, reports of them became familiar sights in daily newspapers during the holiday season, typically under the police report section.

This article appeared in the "Police Intelligence" column of the *New York Herald* in 1837.

Peace of the City.—The peace and good order of the city during this New Year's, has been, we must say, remarkably well kept. Through the activity and vigilance of his honor the Mayor, who was very busily engaged in all parts of the city, giving instructions to his officers for the immediate suppression of any outbreak or riot that might occur. There was certainly an unusual number of Callithumpian bands out, perambulating the streets; but seeing such a strong body of police watching them on every corner, kept them within bounds, and the whole of New Year's eve and the day passed off in a manner creditable to the city. Not even a fire, nor an alarm of one, occurred during the whole time; which, together with the oppressive heat of the day, was, to say the least, two very remarkable facts.

Article from the *New York Herald* reporting callithumpian activity, 1847. SOURCE: LIBRARY OF CONGRESS.

SOURCE: DOROTHY SIEMENS.

CHAPTER 10
A "Breech" of Christmas Spirit
Pant-emonium

Who knew that the humble ivy vine could be the source of such mischievous merrymaking?

Ivy has a long association with Bacchus, the Roman god of wine, and featured in the festivities of the Bacchanalia, the celebration honoring him. It's also commonly associated with death, due to it being a common sight in English cemeteries. And so, because it tended to conjure images of all things pagan, gluttonous, debauched, and morbid, it was eventually forbidden in Christian homes.

Centuries later, though, that symbolism had worn off. The nature of ivy to cling and climb inspired a new symbolism. Ivy was rebranded as an emblem of fidelity and dependence on God for strength. Still, it would be a long time before anybody embraced it as a Christmas decoration. And when the English eventually did, they initially restricted it to outdoor use, favoring holly for the indoors. But by the late Middle Ages, ivy had become a traditional Christmas symbol, and it remains one today. Its revered status was even commemorated in this fifteenth-century carol:

Ivy, Chief of Trees

The most worthy she is in town,
He that saith other, doth amiss;
And worthy to bear the crown;
Veni coronaberis.

Ivy is soft and meek of speech,
Against all bale she is bliss;
Well is he that may her reach,
Veni coronaberis.

Ivy is green with colour bright,
Of all trees best she is;
And that I prove well now be right,
Veni coronaberis.

Ivy beareth berries black.
God grant us all His bliss;
For there shall we nothing lack,
Veni coronaberis.

John Stow, in his 1598 *The Survey of London*, wrote, "Against the feast of Christmas every man's house, as also the parish churches, were decked with holm, ivy, bays, and whatsoever the season of the year afforded to be green. The conduits and standards in the streets were likewise garnished." No English home would be properly prepped for Christmas without ivy. Indeed, to be caught without it was to be caught with your pants down . . . or *up*, in this case.

An 1884 issue of *Harper's New Monthly Magazine* featured reporting of a strange and devious English custom from Christmas past:

> In some places in Oxfordshire, it was the custom for the maid-servant to ask the man for ivy to dress the house, and if the man refused or neglected to fetch the ivy, the maid stole a pair of his breeches and nailed them up to the gate in the garden or highway.

Talk about having your laundry aired in public!

PANTS, THEATER, AND CHRISTMAS
It's All Connected

Those breeches that might get nailed to the gate are related to the history of Christmas in a curious way.

First things first: The word "breeches" today refers to a form of clothing that covers each leg, stopping just below the knee. The first usage of the word referred to *undergarments*. Only later did it refer to both under and outer garments. So we don't know what kind of laundry was being publicly aired for those poor ivy-less Englishmen—either way, we *do* hope it was clean!

Breeches (or "britches," take your pick) were a common form of lower body clothing until the early nineteenth century, when trousers took over.

But Americans don't normally say "trousers," do we? We say "pants." Why? To answer that question, we need to go back to the sixteenth century and the commedia dell'arte, an early form of professional theater originating in Italy. Commedia dell'arte plays featured a character named Pantalone, known for his greed and—getting back to the point—his tightly fitting, full-length leggings.

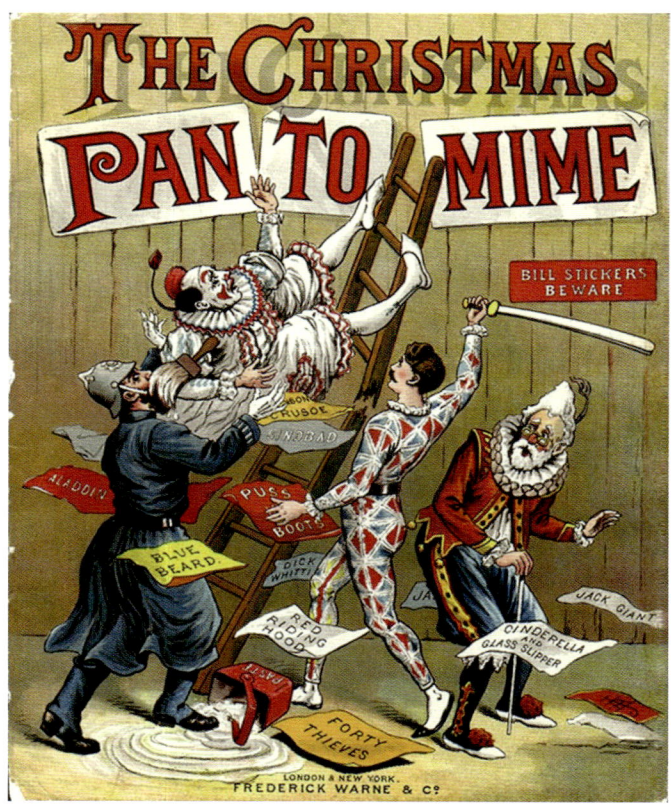

The Christmas Pantomime color lithograph book cover, 1890, showing harlequinade characters. SOURCE: WIKIMEDIA.

A "BREECH" OF CHRISTMAS SPIRIT

Pantalone became *pantalon* in French, which became "pantaloons" in English to refer to an article of clothing with full leg coverage. This was shortened into its final form of simply "pants."

Along the way, a branch of the commedia dell'arte evolved to become the pantomime, featuring similar characters and costumes. And pantomime went on to become a popular form of theater for Christmastime. It has become practically synonymous with theatrical Christmastime entertainment in England and parts of the United States.

Who'd have thought that pants history and Christmas history would be . . . *woven* together?

SOURCE: DOROTHY SIEMENS.

CHAPTER 11

Holly Beating

A Holly Not-So-Jolly Tradition

You better watch out
You better not cry
You better not sleep too late
I'm telling you why
You might get beaten with holly!

At least, you might have if you lived in Wales many years ago. And if you've ever seen a holly sprig close up, with its thick, spiky-edged leaves, you know why you definitely want to avoid that.

The strange tradition of "holly beating" is exactly what it sounds like. On Saint Stephen's Day, young Welshmen were known to haul out the holly in particularly aggressive fashion. Oftentimes, the intent of holly beating (also known as "holming") was to produce welts and even draw blood on the exposed arms and legs of the target.

One way to find yourself on the wrong end of a holly sprig was to be the last one out of bed in the morning. The unfortunate late riser was eligible for a thrashing from other members of the household. Afterward, the sleepyhead might even be made to wait on the rest of the family for the day.

But it wasn't just late sleepers who needed to worry. Holly beaters would also take to the streets. Female servants were especially likely targets if they encountered rascally young men out and about in the village. In some areas, *any* young lady (servant or not) could be the next victim.

Thankfully, holly beating never caught on outside Wales. Truth be told, that's a bit surprising, given the volatile combination of easily accessible holly and boys being boys. The practice mercifully died out toward the end of the nineteenth century.

HOLLY BEATING

THE HOLLY TREE INN
The Winter of His Discontent

"May the green Holly-Tree flourish, striking its roots deep into our English ground, and having its germinating qualities carried by the birds of Heaven all over the world."
—Charles Dickens, "The Holly Tree Inn"

If the idea of beatings with a branch of holly don't get you into the Christmas spirit, how about a Christmas story that takes place at an inn called the Holly Tree?

"The Holly Tree Inn" first appeared in an 1855 bonus issue of *Household Words*, a weekly magazine edited by Charles Dickens. It was later republished in various other collections. It consists of several short stories by different authors, contained within a main story written by Dickens himself.

In the story, Charley is a shy Londoner who believes that his fiancée Angela is having an affair with his best friend, Edwin. Charley decides to flee to America, but en route to the port he encounters a storm and takes refuge at a Yorkshire inn called the Holly Tree. He finds himself in that now familiar plotline of being snowed in, just days before Christmas.

Charley is bored and lonely at the inn, and he spends his time reminiscing about his extensive experience traveling to inns in England, Wales, France, Italy, and America. He shares how his first memories about inns were from horror stories that a caretaker told him in his early childhood. He recounts the stories of an evil innkeeper who murdered his guests, a burglar who lost an ear while breaking and entering,

THE HOLLY TREE INN
AND
A CHRISTMAS TREE

AS WRITTEN IN THE CHRISTMAS STORIES
BY CHARLES DICKENS

WITH ILLUSTRATIONS IN COLOUR AND LINE BY
GEORGE ALFRED WILLIAMS

NEW YORK
THE BAKER & TAYLOR COMPANY
Publishers

Title page from a 1907 edition of "The Holly Tree Inn." SOURCE: LIBRARY OF CONGRESS.

and a parrot who tipped a guest off about a murder at the inn.

Having relived all these memories, Charley decides to overcome his shyness and talk to the staff at the inn to see whether the Holly Tree has any stories of its own. What follows are five separate stories, involving child runaways, an attempted murder, a mother whose son is accused of murder, and a story about the significance of inns, told in rhyming verse.

The main story concludes when, a couple of days after Christmas, the roads are finally cleared and Charley settles up at the inn. He's about to depart from the Holly Tree when a coach pulls up and Edwin steps out. It turns out the whole thing was a misunderstanding: Edwin was actually in love with Angela's cousin Emmeline. Charley returns to London to marry Angela.

Portrait of Charles Dickens, circa 1867.
SOURCE: WIKIMEDIA COMMONS.

SOURCE: DOROTHY SIEMENS.

CHAPTER 12
Blowing the Christmas Pudding
Fire When Ready

The Christmas pudding, that dense and delicious pièce de résistance of many a Christmas dinner, is a feast for the senses—including the sense of hearing.

In a scene from *A Christmas Carol*, Charles Dickens describes Tiny Tim being brought "off into the wash-house, that he might hear the pudding singing in the copper." The "singing" refers to the sound of steam released as the pudding boils in its cloth wrapper in the Cratchits' copper washbasin.

There's also the rushing sound of fire when the pudding is doused in brandy and set alight in blue flames. And, of course, there's the traditional round of applause that greets the pudding when it's ceremoniously brought to the table.

But if you happened to celebrate Christmas in Newfoundland long ago, one other sound accompanied the Christmas pudding: gunfire!

It's Christmas Day on Horse Islands, a pair of islands off the coast of Newfoundland in the Labrador Sea. The lady of the house is about to perform an important task: it's time to lift the pudding from the pot. And whereas Mrs. Cratchit "left the room alone—too nervous to bear witness—to take the pudding up, and bring it in," our Canadian friend has no such luxury. The man of the house is watching, standing outside the backdoor of the house. Once the pudding is out, he'll fire his gun into the air—a triumphant one-gun salute to Christmas.

Celebratory gunfire has a long (and dangerous) history and was common in the eighteenth and nineteenth centuries. These *feux de joie*—French for "fires of joy"—might celebrate the New Year, visiting dignitaries, victories, weddings, funerals, or, as in this case, the arrival of Christmas at last.

This strange Canadian Christmas custom went by names like "blowing the Christmas pudding" or "shooting out the pudding" and has mercifully died out.

BLOWING THE CHRISTMAS PUDDING

HAVE YOURSELF A NOISY LITTLE CHRISTMAS

Rootin'-Tootin' Revelry

Where would Christmas be without many of the inventions of everyday life? Try to imagine a Christmas season without electric lights, recorded music, or modern transportation. One invention even older than any of these probably doesn't spring to mind when you think of Christmas. And yet it does have a quirky connection: gunpowder.

Invented sometime in the first millennium, gunpowder undeniably changed the world. And for many throughout history (including up to the present day), it has changed Christmas . . . or at least how Christmas sounds.

The idea of using gunfire or fireworks to herald the season is known as "shooting in" Christmas. This practice likely evolved from ancient traditions in which loud noises were made to scare off evil spirits. In addition to Newfoundland's blowing the Christmas pudding, here are some explosive Christmas customs from around the world.

> *United States:* The Appalachian Christmas tradition of serenading involves groups of costumed young people going door to door on Christmas Eve, making as much noise as possible. This often includes firecrackers and gunshots.
>
> In New Mexico, the Christmas Eve Procession of the Virgin Mary at Taos Pueblo's San Geronimo Church includes rifle shots every thirty seconds, while the church bell clangs.

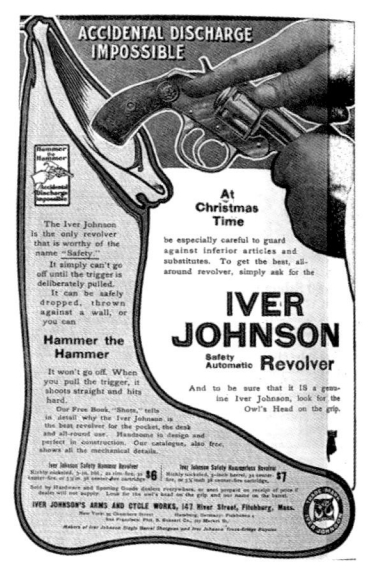

In early twentieth-century newspapers and magazines, guns were commonly advertised as Christmas gifts. SOURCE: HATHI TRUST.

Germany: Since at least as early as 1666, groups of marksmen have fired traditional black powder guns from hilltops at midnight on Christmas Eve.

Norway: In rural areas of Norway, young men brought their guns from farm to farm on Christmas Eve. John Oscar Hall describes the tradition in his 1921 memoir *When I Was a Boy in Norway*:

> The young men go from farm to farm and sneak up close to the window while shooting, in order to make the people quake. But they could not be offended, as such a visit was considered an honor, and the husbandman would go and invite them in for refreshments.

Ireland: There was a time in Ireland when tradition called for a gun salute at noon on Christmas Eve.

Germany: Beginning on December 17, the Christ child is heralded with a combination of church bells and rifle fire. Between 11:30 p.m. and midnight, the gunfire increases, as a reminder for everyone to get to midnight mass.

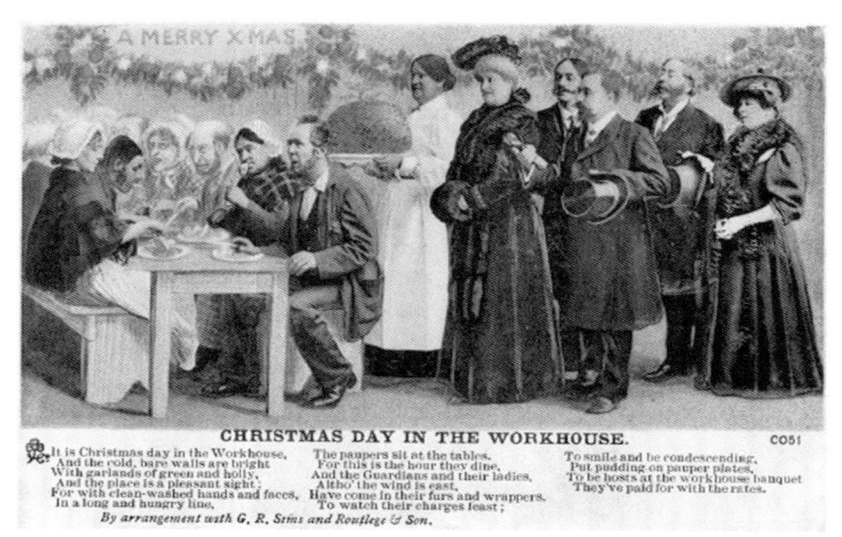

Postcard circa 1900 showing Christmas charity given in a workhouse. SOURCE: WIKIMEDIA COMMONS.

PART 4
Money and Charity

Retail shopping hasn't always dominated the Christmas season. But for much of its history, there has been an expectation that certain people would be spending money in various ways. That relationship between Christmas and money has always changed with the times and the ever-shifting economic landscape. From door-to-door begging to creative banking, money and charity are part of the rich (and poor) history of Christmas.

SOURCE: DOROTHY SIEMENS.

CHAPTER 13

Begging Visits
We Won't Go Until We Get Some

Those singers demanding, "Now bring us some figgy pudding and bring some out here," weren't only singing the praises of that dense, boozy steamed cake. They were also illustrating how Christmas past was a time when people went door to door, soliciting charity and hospitality.

Back in the Middle Ages, charity mainly flowed from the monarchy and the church. King Henry III famously fed thousands of poor people at his palace in 1248. Medieval monasteries and nunneries also made special allowance for increased giving at Christmastime. In time, owners of large landed estates were also expected to show generosity at Christmastime. As a result, it eventually became common—and, importantly, *allowed*—for people to form roving bands for the purpose of soliciting charity.

These "begging visits" usually involved some kind of performance—a song, verse, or drama—or sometimes a blessing, in exchange for money, food, or drink. They could also involve costumes, as with the visitors who dressed as the Magi and went roving on Twelfth

Nineteenth-century English Christmas card showing carol singers.
SOURCE: THE BRITISH MUSEUM.

Night (see also WREN DAY, THE MARI LWYD, and THE BROAD). Begging visits were common throughout the twelve days of Christmas, with traditions unique to Twelfth Night, New Year's Eve, Christmas Eve, and Christmas Day.

Sometimes begging visits resembled modern trick-or-treating, with the threat of a curse or prank for those who refused to provide charity.

Not all Christmastime door-to-door visiting took the form of a begging visit. Sometimes the aim was purely social and festive, like wassailing—basically, a boozier version of caroling.

Begging visits have been an on-again, off-again custom throughout Christmas history. Some forms still exist today (see WREN DAY), but the money collected usually goes to an established charity.

BEGGING VISITS

A SHORT HISTORY OF CHRISTMAS CHARITY
The Season of Giving

Whether it's those street-corner bell ringers for the Salvation Army or solicitations received in the mail, the Christmas season is filled with appeals to our charitable nature.

The season is a perfect mix. The general feelings of warmth and affection toward one and all. The free flow of spending. And the impossible-to-ignore contrast between the luxurious excess of the season and the various ways that many people struggle to meet their basic needs. Or, as one of the charity collectors said to Scrooge in *A Christmas Carol*, "It is a time, of all others, when want is keenly felt, and abundance rejoices."

Modern Christmas charity is usually organized by a charitable group and funded by donations from individuals (like you and me) or larger entities (like corporations). This is a relatively new idea.

The Christmas charity from the monarchy and church that began in the Middle Ages faded out in the seventeenth century. Interest in Christmas charity generally was in decline around then, as was Christmas itself. During this period Protestant reformers suppressed Christmas celebrations in England, Scotland, and the Massachusetts Bay Colony. This decline was enough to prompt one poet to lament that "Christmas bread and beef is turned into stones" and that "lady money" sleeps in "misers' bags" (see poem on the next page).

We can thank the Victorians for reviving the idea of Christmas charity. Not only did they make it part of the season again, but they also changed how it was given out and by whom. Rather than the monarchy or the church doing the giving, individual donors were asked to open their hearts and wallets. This approach forms the basis of most modern Christmas charity.

This poem was published anonymously in 1612.

A Song Bewailing the Time of Christmas, So Much Decayed in England

Christmas is my name, far have I gone, have I gone, have I gone, have I gone without regard,
Whereas great men, by flocks they be flown, they be flown, they be flown, they be flown to London ward,
Where they in pomp and pleasure do waste that which Christmas had wont to feast;
    Wellay day.
Houses where music was wonted to ring,
Nothing but bats, and owls now do sing
Wellay day, wellay day, wellay day, where should I stay.

Christmas bread and beef is turned into stones, into stones, into stones,
Into stones and silken rags.
And lady money it doth sleep, it doth sleep, it doth sleep,
It doth sleep in misers' bags.
Where many gallants once abound,

BEGGING VISITS

Nought but a dog and a shepherd is found,
       Wellay day.
Places where Christmas revels did keep,
Are now become habitations for sheep.
Wellay day, wellay day, wellay day, where should I stay.

Pan, the shepherd's god, doth deface, doth deface, doth deface, doth deface,
    Lady Ceres' crown,
And tilliges doth decay, doth decay, doth decay, doth decay in every town.
Landlords their rents so highly enhance,
That Peares the plowman barefoot doth dance,
       Wellay day.

       Farmers that Christmas would entertain,
hath scarcely withal them selves to maintain,
Wellay day, wellay day, wellay day, where should I stay.

Go to the Protestant, he'll protest, he'll protest, he'll protest,
he will protest and boldly boast,
And to the Puritan, he is so hot, he is so hot, he is so hot, he is so hot he will
    burn the roast,
The Catholic good deeds will not scorn,
nor will not see poor Christmas forlorn,
       Wellay day.
Since Holiness no good deeds will do,
Protestants had best turn Papists too,
Wellay day, wellay day, wellay day, where should I stay.

Pride and Luxury doth devour, doth devour, doth devour,
doth devour house keeping quite,
And beggary doth beget, doth beget, doth beget,
doth beget in many a knight.
Madam for sooth in coach she must reel
Although she wear her house out a heel,
    Wellay day.
And on her back were that for her weed,
that would both me, and many other feed,
Wellay day, wellay day, wellay day, where should I stay.

Briefly for to end, here I find, here I find,
here I find such great vacation
That some great houses do seem to have, seem to have,
    seem to have,
for to have some great purgation,
With purging pills, such effects they have showed,
that out of doors, their owners they have spewed.
    Wellay day.
And when Christmas goes by and calls,
Nothing but solitude, and naked walls,
Wellay day, wellay day, wellay day, where should I stay.

Pilemel's cottages are turned into gold, into gold,
Into gold for harboring Jove.
And great men's houses up for to hold, up for to hold, up for to hold, make
    great men moan,

BEGGING VISITS

But in the city they say they do live,
Where gold by handfuls away they do give,
    Wellay day.
There therefore thither I purpose to pass,
hoping at London to find the golden ass,
I'll away, I'll away, I'll no longer stay.

SOURCE: DOROTHY SIEMENS.

CHAPTER 14
Saving at the Pub
Christmas Is Coming, the Goose Is Getting Fat

All that Christmas merrymaking—the gifts, food, drink, and travel—comes with a hefty price tag. In the early twentieth century, banks and credit unions began offering "Christmas clubs," savings accounts specifically for Christmas savings. Customers would make weekly deposits and withdraw the money (with its accrued interest) at Christmastime.

Up until the Great Depression, Christmas clubs were hugely successful. They were good PR for the banks, and evidently many people found it useful to keep their Christmas money separate.

The idea may have been inspired by factories that set up similar programs for their employees. Whichever one came first, it was merely an institutionalized version of a much older (and less formal) idea from Victorian England: the goose club.

For many, it's hard to imagine a Christmas dinner without a roasted turkey at its center. In *A Christmas Carol*, Scrooge's first order of business after changing his miserly ways is to buy the prize turkey from the poulterer for the Cratchit family. Charles Dickens is often credited with helping to popularize the turkey for Christmas dinner, because, at the time of his writing, the goose was still the common Christmas meal for working-class Victorian families.

Goose clubs were organized by village pubs or markets. The basic idea was the same as the banks' Christmas clubs: participants made small deposits throughout the year. By Christmastime, they had saved enough for a Christmas feast. In many cases, the pub owner raised the geese behind the pub.

Like the modern Christmas club, the goose club took a sterile, commercial transaction (i.e., making savings deposits) and gave it a sheen of festivity and anticipation for the coming season. Not only that, but it also fostered a sense of community Christmas spirit as only a village pub can. Goose clubs often also included a raffle for the prize bird or alcohol, adding to the excitement.

NUMISMATIC NICHOLAS
Dollars and Saints

These days, it can seem like Christmas is all about the money. But there was a time when money was all about the Christmas.

In the days before the federal government issued paper money, private banks issued their own. Privately issued banknotes came in a wide variety of designs and denominations and often featured stock images provided by the printing companies hired to do the engraving. Several banks used images of none other than Saint Nicholas.

A total of twenty-one banks from eight states—including the aptly named Saint Nicholas Bank of New York—issued currency featuring the jolly saint. According to the American Numismatic

SAVING AT THE PUB

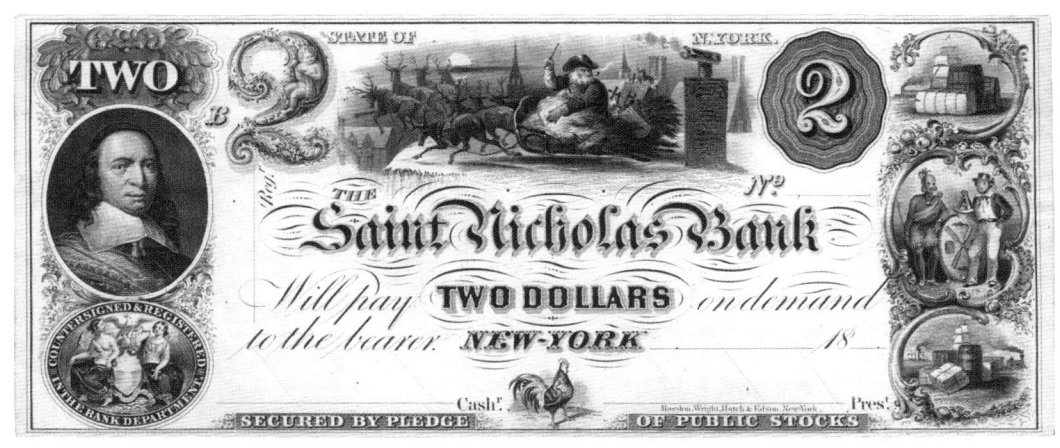

SOURCE: AMERICAN NUMISMATIC ASSOCIATION.

Association ("numismatics" being the study of coins and paper money), there are twenty-seven known examples of banknotes bearing the likeness of Saint Nicholas. All of these banknotes were issued in the mid-nineteenth century. This was a time when the image of Santa Claus was quickly transforming in America, due to the influence of Dutch settlers in New York and the writings of Washington Irving and Clement Clarke Moore. An image shown on many banknotes depicted Nicholas riding a reindeer-pulled sleigh across housetops—a new idea at the time.

These old banknotes are now highly sought-after collector's items. A five-dollar banknote from the Howard Bank of Massachusetts fetched over $8,000 at auction in 2012.

SOURCE: DOROTHY SIEMENS.

CHAPTER 15

Wren Day

Animal Sacrifice Meets Christmas Spirit Meets Fund-Raising

The small but mighty wren: they're some of the tiniest birds in existence, and their plumage may be drab, but just wait until they start singing. Their loud, complex songs and their tendency to sing them throughout winter have earned them the title "King of Birds."

But on Saint Stephen's Day, the king is dead.

From Ireland and the Isle of Man comes the custom of Wren Day. Men and boys would hunt for a wren by beating around the furze bushes they perched in. As the spooked wrens flew off, the "wren boys" would throw rocks and sticks to try to strike one down. It was considered good luck to be the wren boy who dealt the fatal blow.

The wren was then mounted on the top of a staff decorated with holly, ivy, and ribbons. An elaborate procession followed. The wren boys dressed in straw masks and motley patterned (think court-jester style) clothing and paraded around the neighborhood. They'd go door to door singing songs and playing music for money. There are several variations of "The Wren Song," including this one:

> *The wren, the wren, the king of all birds,*
> *St. Stephen's Day was caught in the furze,*
> *Although he was little his honour was great,*
> *Jump up me lads and give him a treat.*
>
> *Chorus:*
> *Up with the kettle and down with the pan,*
> *And give us a penny to bury the wren.*

On the Isle of Man, the wren boys completed the ritual with a funeral for the wren.

All of this fuss raises an obvious question: Why? The exact origins are unknown, though theories and legends abound, including the one about Saint Stephen, who, hiding from his enemies in a furze, had his cover blown by a noisy wren. However, the real answer is likely that the tradition combines ancient Celtic rituals and superstitions that simply carried over into Christmas.

Fortunately for our feathered friends, the custom died out by the nineteenth century. While some version of Wren Day exists today (revived starting in the late twentieth century), a replica of a wren is used, and the money is collected for charity.

WREN DAY

CHRISTMAS IS FOR THE BIRDS
Fine Feathered Festivity

Have you ever stopped to think of the role that birds play in Christmas? Many a Christmas card design features a bright red cardinal in a wintry landscape. Six of the gifts in the song "The Twelve Days of Christmas" are birds. These days, penguins are increasingly popular as tree ornaments and lawn decorations. And let's not forget the centerpiece of a traditional Christmas dinner: a turkey.

Here are some more bird-related Christmas traditions and legends, past and present. In keeping with the theme of this section of the book, many of these traditions are charitable toward our fine feathered friends.

> *Christmas bird count:* Every year since 1900, birdwatchers in the Americas have participated in the Christmas bird count between December 14 and January 5. This event helps track important information about bird populations.
>
> *Birds at the Nativity:* According to legend, a stork was present at the inn where Jesus was born and plucked out its feathers to line the manger. The robin is said to have used its wings to fan the flames in order to keep the baby warm. And a nightingale sang the baby to sleep.
>
> *Birdfeeders, Christmas style:* In Norway, tradition calls for a sheaf of grain (typically wheat or oats) set on a pole for birds on Christmas morning. This offering is known as a *julenek*.

Christmas card featuring a robin, 1908. SOURCE: NEW YORK PUBLIC LIBRARY.

Carol of the birds: A Spanish carol tells a version of the Nativity story in which a nightingale, sparrow, and partridge sing praise to the newborn baby on the appearance of the Christmas Star in the night sky.

Bride's tree: A bride's tree is a kind of Christmas tree from Bavaria. Twelve ornaments are hung on it, each one symbolizing something necessary for a happy marriage. The bird ornament symbolizes joy.

Dead birds: Christmas cards ain't what they used to be. Many early examples from Victorian England featured creepy or morbid images. Dead robins and sparrows were quite common.

Putting the old tree to good use: Some observe a tradition that, when the tree is taken down (see UNDECKING THE HALLS), it is put outside and hung with food for birds.

The fortune-telling goose: Here's an example from the rich history of believing that Christmastime was the season for divining the future—especially one's romantic future. In an old German tradition, girls would blindfold a goose. The first girl the goose bumped into would be the next to find a husband.

A family burns their Christmas greenery after Christmas. Illustration from *Harper's Weekly*, 1876.
SOURCE: HATHI TRUST.

PART 5

Keeping House

There's no place like home for the holidays. But what does a well-kept home mean at Christmastime? It depends on whom (and when and where) you ask. In this section, we explore a couple of holiday housekeeping notions with ancient roots.

SOURCE: DOROTHY SIEMENS.

CHAPTER 16
Undecking the Halls
Timing Is Everything

How long should you keep the Christmas decorations up? These days, there's a pretty simple answer. Right after Thanksgiving, up go the tree and the lights. The halls are decked, and all is merry and bright for around five weeks. Then, just after New Year's Day, everything gets packed away for another year, and the dried-out tree gets kicked to the curb for trash day. Throughout history, though, there have been many accepted deadlines for undecking the halls.

Some have observed the date as Twelfth Night (January 5) or even as late as Candlemas (February 2). In between is Saint Knut's Day on January 13. This Swedish and Finnish celebration honors Canute Lavard, a twelfth-century Danish nobleman who later became a saint.

Many people still observe Saint Knut's Day today as the day of undecking, but not the same way their ancestors did. In olden times, on Saint Knut's Day, people would tap the household walls with sticks to chase away lurking Christmas ghosts and trolls. They'd also open their windows and doors to sweep out any remnants of Christmas decorating.

Tapping on the walls wasn't the only safeguard against spooky Christmas creatures and misfortune. Many traditions called for not only removing Christmas greenery from the home on a specific date but also burning it. The seventeenth-century poet Robert Herrick even wrote that the neglectful householder would be tormented by goblins, the number of which would equal the number of leaves left unburned.

> *Down with the rosemary, and so*
> *Down with the bales of mistletoe;*
> *Down with the holly, ivie, all*
> *Wherewith ye drest the Christmas hall;*
>
> *That so the superstitious find*
> *No one least branch left there behind;*
> *For look, how many leaves there be*
> *Neglected there, maids, trust to me,*
> *So many goblins you shall see.*

THE CRICKET ON THE HEARTH
Chirping and Cheer

Speaking of Christmastime superstitions, it was once considered good luck for a cricket to chirp at Christmastime. Crickets have long been associated with luck in many cultures. Naturally, they have found their way into Christmas lore, as in the 1958 animated special *From All of Us to All of You* (later retitled *Jiminy Cricket's Christmas*) and the 1973 animated special *A Very Merry Cricket*. But before any of that, there was Charles Dickens's 1845 novella *The Cricket on the Hearth: A Fairy Tale of Home*.

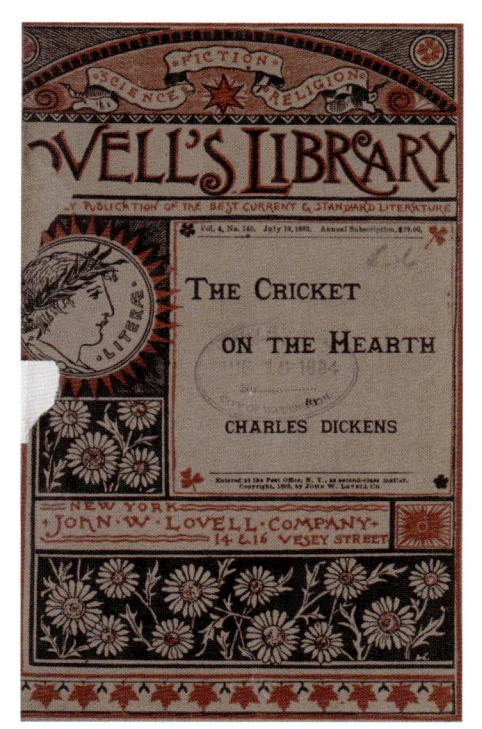

Cover from an 1883 edition of *The Cricket on the Hearth*. SOURCE: LIBRARY OF CONGRESS.

The story came about after Dickens abandoned his idea of creating a periodical about domestic matters called *The Cricket*. He reworked the idea into a fantasy story set in a family's home. It is considered one of Dickens's five Christmas books, along with *A Christmas Carol*, *The Chimes*, *The Battle of Life*, and *The Haunted Man*. However, *The Cricket on the Hearth* is a departure from Dickens's other well-known Christmas stories, which include elements of the supernatural and social commentary. In addition, the story takes place in January and doesn't actually involve Christmas. (For Dickens, "Christmas books" were those published *for* the Christmas season and not necessarily *about* Christmas.)

In the story, the cricket lives on the hearth in the home of John Peerybingle and his much younger wife, Dot. The cricket is part guardian angel, part indicator of household happiness. When things are going well, the cricket chirps; when they aren't, it is silent.

A jealous old toy merchant misleads John into believing that Dot has been unfaithful. But in response, the cricket's chirping becomes a form of magic, causing John to see visions of Dot's loyalty and goodness and ultimately leading to a happy ending.

The Cricket on the Hearth was a major commercial success and adapted many times for stage and screen, including the 1967 Rankin/Bass animated special.

SOURCE: DOROTHY SIEMENS.

CHAPTER 17
First-Footing
Best Foot Forward

It's the wee hours of Christmas morning in Montenegro, sometime in the distant past. The large Yule log in the fireplace, set afire as part of the Vigil of the Nativity, is nearly burned down. There's a knock at the door. Answering the door, we find a man standing outside, holding one of his gloves in his hand. In the glove is kernels, which he sprinkles over the threshold as he says, "Christ is born." A member of the household then sprinkles some of the corn over the man, answering, "He is born indeed."

The man is then invited inside, where he goes to the nearly extinguished Yule log and pokes it to send sparks flying. As he does so, he recites a blessing of good luck for the household. Sometimes money, an orange, or both are placed on the log to seal the blessing.

So what's all this about? The family, of course, was expecting the man to visit. And, importantly, they made sure no other guests arrived first. The man was known as a *polaznik*. And sometimes he brought wheat or even a loaf of bread instead of corn. He was carrying out an old custom that placed great importance on the first person to enter a home on Christmas or New Year's Day. The fortunes of the entire household were staked on this visit, and the *polaznik* was performing a role to ensure only good fortune.

The custom is known as "first-footing." And many cultures in eastern and western Europe and Great Britain have put their own spin on it. Generally, first-footing was a boys' club; it was considered unlucky for a woman to be the first across the threshold on these occasions. Sometimes the physical appearance of the first footer mattered too. Dark-haired men were often considered especially lucky; other times, blondes had all the fun. (Redheads were unanimously a no-no.) Unmarried men were also considered lucky.

First-footing was too important to leave to fate. Families would specially coordinate the first footer, sometimes even hiring a man who ticked all the good-luck boxes to pay a visit after midnight. First-footing is still in practice today in Scotland for the New Year's celebration of Hogmanay.

OTHER CHRISTMAS FIRSTS
Every Tradition Had to Start Somewhere

First-footing isn't the only thing about Christmas to do with being first. The long history of Christmas includes countless firsts, like these:

336: For the first time, Christmas is observed on December 25.

567: The Council of Tours establishes the twelve days of Christmas from December 25 to January 5.

1223: The first living nativity scene, attributed to Saint Francis of Assisi, appears in Greccio, Italy.

1583: Scotland bans Christmas, perhaps the world's first such ban. Reformers had been pushing for decades, citing that the Bible does not call for Christmas celebrations. The ban would last nearly four hundred years.

1773: The first printed mention of the name "Santa Claus" (anglicized from the Dutch *Sinterklaas*) appears in a New York newspaper.

1818: "Silent Night" is sung for the first time.

1843: The first commercially produced Christmas card is printed, commissioned by Englishman Sir Henry Cole and designed by John Horsley.

1853: President Franklin Pierce has the first White House Christmas tree.

The world's first commercially produced Christmas card, designed by John Callcott Horsley for Henry Cole in 1843. SOURCE: WIKIPEDIA.

1890: Retailer James Edgar dresses as Santa Claus for shoppers at his Brockton, Massachusetts, store, introducing the concept of the department store Santa.

1898: Canada issues the world's first Christmas postage stamp. (The United States wouldn't issue its own until 1962.)

1924: Macy's holds its first Thanksgiving Day parade, forever reshaping the American Christmas season.

1965: Astronauts on NASA's Gemini 6 broadcast the first song from space: "Jingle Bells."

CHRISTMAS THROUGHOUT CHRISTENDOM.

THE CHRIST-CHILD AND HANS TRAPP.

Illustration from *Harper's Weekly*, 1872. SOURCE: LIBRARY OF CONGRESS.

PART 6
Gift Bringers

Santa lives in the North Pole and spends the year keeping track of naughty and nice boys and girls and making toys with his workforce of elves. On Christmas Eve, he flies from house to house in his reindeer-pulled sleigh, delivering gifts, one chimney hop at a time. And that's the way it's been since, oh, the late nineteenth century. But before that? Jolly old Saint Nick wasn't the only game in town. Christmas history is filled with a ragtag cast of characters who have stepped into the gift-bringer role or that of the gift bringer's companion. From gruff, threatening tramps to horned demons, it's Christmas gift bringing as you've (thankfully) never seen it before!

SOURCE: DOROTHY SIEMENS.

CHAPTER 18
The Saint's Surly Servants
So Be Good, for Goodness' Sake!

These days, warning children that they'd better not shout, cry, or pout doesn't carry much weight. The "threat" is merely that Santa Claus is coming to town, and the maximum sentence for naughty children—though hardly ever carried out—is a lump of coal.

The image of Santa Claus as a right jolly old elf who works alone on Christmas Eve is relatively new. Back when he was still plain old Saint Nicholas, he could be more of a stern disciplinary figure. But it wasn't exactly saintly to mete out punishments. So, for that, he engaged in the old "good cop, bad cop" routine with a cast of surly characters. Coming from different European traditions, these characters accompanied him on his Christmas gift bringing to dole out beatings, kidnappings, and, yes, the occasional lump of coal.

Krampus, a horned devil, threatened to hit naughty children with a stick or throw them into the basket he went around with. Klaubauf and Čert were similar characters, Klaubauf being a shaggy monster and Čert a tar-covered devil.

There were also Rough Nicholas, Furry Nicholas, and Nicholas in Ashes. These gruff and grizzled characters were like Saint Nicholas's evil twin brothers, often wearing tattered clothing and usually carrying a birch rod for naughty children. Farmhand Rupert, Hans Trapp, and Father Whipper (or his American equivalent, Father Flog) were rough ragamuffins cut from the same cloth.

Black Pete is a figure originally from Dutch folklore. Though not typically portrayed as shaggy, he did similar bidding as Nicholas's other companions.

Luckily for children, in most cases, Saint Nicholas honored his role as good cop, stepping in before any gruesome threats could be carried out.

THE SAINT'S SURLY SERVANTS

THE ART OF CHRISTMAS NIGHTMARES

Santa's Enforcers in Print

Saint Nicholas's companions weren't only the stuff of stern parents' warnings or scary bedtime stories. They often appeared in various pieces of visual media, like paintings, greeting cards, and illustrations in newspapers and children's books.

Painting by Nikolaus Hoffmann, circa 1760, showing Farmhand Rupert at a family Christmas celebration. SOURCE: WIKIMEDIA COMMONS.

Panel from a nineteenth-century print, showing Father Flog.
SOURCE: YALE UNIVERSITY ART GALLERY.

He takes home with him those who are disobedient.

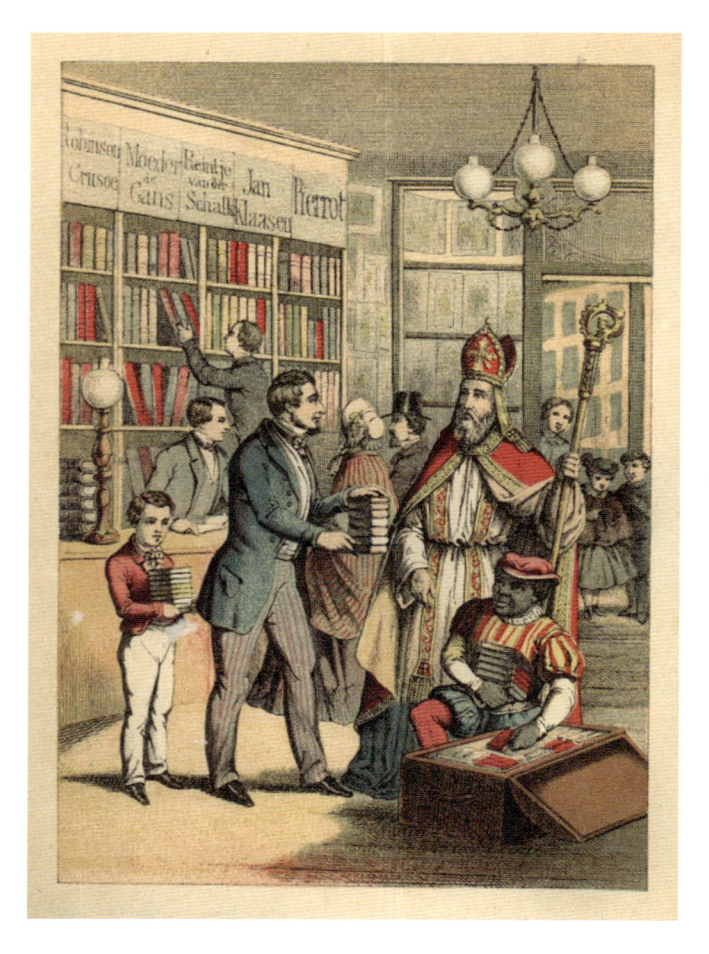

Illustration from an 1880 book showing Saint Nicholas with Black Pete. SOURCE: WIKIPEDIA.

Early twentieth-century illustration of Saint Nicholas and Krampus visiting a child.
SOURCE: WIKIPEDIA.

SOURCE: DOROTHY SIEMENS.

CHAPTER 19
Baby Jesus, Gift Bringer
Happy Birthday, Jesus! What Did You Get Me?

Being Santa Claus is a tough job, and old Saint Nick has weathered some ups and downs over his career—including a demotion in the sixteenth century. Up until then, Saint Nicholas had been a traditional holiday gift bringer, but *not* at Christmas. Instead, he made his rounds on December 6: Saint Nicholas Day. But then along came the Protestant Reformation.

Devotion to saints amounted to idolatry in the eyes of Martin Luther and his followers. And so, to distance themselves from the saints, Protestants abandoned the celebration of Saint Nicholas Day. Of course, many of them were reluctant to give up the idea of a gift-giving occasion, so they adopted Christmas Eve as an acceptable alternative. Now all they needed was a new gift bringer that Protestants could get behind. And what better choice than Jesus himself?

Christkindl (alternatively, *Christkind*) means "the Christ child." Christkindl was a character initially pictured as the baby Jesus. Over time, though, that image evolved into something more like the angelic children of Renaissance art. He was pictured wearing a white robe and crown, with angel's wings.

Christkindl became the traditional gift bringer in Austria, Switzerland, and southern and western Germany. According to legend, he entered houses unseen to leave gifts for children. When his work was done and he was safely out of sight, he rang a small bell alerting the family to go to the living room to find the gifts. He often traveled with a companion, just like Saint Nicholas did (see THE SAINT'S SURLY SERVANTS).

But some people just couldn't bear to let go of their beloved Saint Nicholas—Reformation or no Reformation. And so, eventually, some believed that Saint Nicholas and Christkindl would deliver gifts *together* on Christmas Eve. This is how Saint Nicholas became part of Christmas. (He never abandoned Saint Nicholas Day, though. To this day, many cultures continue to celebrate December 6 in his honor.) This is also how some people—conflating the figures of Saint Nicholas and Christkindl—eventually mutated the name Christkindl into that familiar nickname for Nicholas: Kris Kringle.

Today, Christkindl remains the main gift bringer in some countries. And many countries hold Christmas street markets called *Christkindl* markets. The *Christkindlmarkt* in Nuremburg, Germany, is the most famous in the world.

CHRISTKINDL ON CHRISTMAS EVE
Oh, Holy Night

Though Christkindl sometimes traveled solo on Christmas Eve delivering gifts, other times he had a traveling companion.

Illustration from the German journal *Die Gartenlaube*, 1891. SOURCE: WIKIMEDIA COMMONS.

Nineteenth-century illustration of Knecht Ruprecht and Christkindl visiting a child.
SOURCE: WIKIMEDIA COMMONS.

Illustration of the Christ child and Hans Trapp.
SOURCE: WIKIMEDIA COMMONS.

Christmas card from 1900 with Saint Nicholas and Christkindl delivering gifts together.
SOURCE: WIKIMEDIA COMMONS.

Newspaper illustration of Christkindl delivering gifts, 1910. SOURCE: LIBRARY OF CONGRESS.

SOURCE: DOROTHY SIEMENS.

CHAPTER 20

Grandfather Frost

Happy New Year, Comrade

You've heard of the goddess of spring and Old Man Winter. They're the physical embodiments of the seasons they're named for. Less familiar are figures like Áine, the goddess of summer, and Shruisthia, the god of autumn. And a certain character from ancient Slavic mythology named Ded Moroz might also have remained lesser known if it hadn't been for the creation of the Soviet Union.

Ded Moroz (Grandfather Frost) came from the same folkloric tradition that forged the images of Father Christmas and Santa Claus. He wears a floor-length fur robe, carries an ornate staff, has a long white beard, and is often shown riding a troika, a horse-drawn sled. But in contrast to Santa's saintly origin story, Ded Moroz was said to be a god—and often a cruel and capricious one at that. He could freeze people and landscapes by snapping his fingers. The Russian Orthodox Church considered him a pagan god.

Over time he became increasingly associated with Christmas in Russia (held on January 7, in accordance with the Julian Calendar), as well as with the character of Snegorotchka (the Snow Maiden) from Russian fairy tales. Snegorotchka is alternately described as the granddaughter or niece of Ded Moroz.

Under the newly formed Russian Communist regime in the early twentieth century, all religion and all religious symbols and celebrations were banned. Ded Moroz found himself in the crosshairs.

But in 1935, Joseph Stalin temporarily lifted the ban on celebrations in an attempt to boost his own popularity and cool tensions after years of unpopular policies. Only New Year's celebrations were allowed so as to avoid any appearance of religiosity. And Ded Moroz in particular was made the public face of the celebration, as a non-Christmassy Christmas gift bringer.

Ded Moroz remains a popular figure in Russian culture today, though his strange stint as the "Soviet Santa" now belongs to Christmas past.

SNEGOROTCHKA
A Fairy Tale of the Allied Nations

Tree ornaments in the likeness of Snegorotchka had been part of Russian Christmases since the late Russian Empire. In the 1930s, when New Year's celebrations were again allowed in Russia, Snegorotchka returned, assuming the role of Ded Moroz's granddaughter and helper.

But prior to any of that, she was a fairytale character, first appearing in the nineteenth century.

The following story appeared in the 1916 collection *Edmund Dulac's Fairy-Book: Fairy Tales of the Allied Nations*.

SNEGOROTCHKA: A RUSSIAN FAIRY TALE

The old wife sang merrily as she sat in the inglenook stirring the soup, for she had never felt so sad. Many, many years had come and gone, leaving the weight of their winters on her shoulders and the touch of snow on her hair without ever bringing her a little child. This made her and her dear old husband very sad, for there were many children outside, playing in the snow. It seemed hard that not even one among them was their very own. But alas! there was no hope for such a blessing now. Never would they see a little fur cap hanging on the corner of the mantelpiece, nor two little shoes drying by the fire.

The old husband brought in a bundle of wood and set it down. Then, as he heard the children laughing and clapping their hands outside, he looked out at the window. There they were, dancing with glee round a snow man they had made. He smiled as he saw that it was evidently meant to look like the Mayor of the village, it was so fat and pompous.

"Look, Marusha!" he cried to the old wife. "Come and see the snow man they've made."

As they stood together at the window, they laughed to see what fun the children got out of it. Suddenly the old man turned to her with a bright idea.

"Let's go out and see if *we* can't make a little snow man."

But Marusha laughed at him. "What would the neighbours say? They would poke fun at us; it'd be the joke of the village. Besides, we're too old to play like children."

"But only a little one, Marusha; only a teeny-weeny little snow man,—and I'll manage it that nobody sees us."

"Well, well," she said, laughing; "have your own way, as you always did, Youshko."

With this she took the pot from the fire, put on her bonnet, and they went out together. As they passed the children, they stopped to play with them a while, for they now felt almost like children themselves.

Snow Maiden, oil painting by Viktor Vasnetsov, 1899. SOURCE: WIKIPEDIA.

Then they trudged on through the snow till they came to a clump of trees, and, behind this, where the snow was nice and white, and nobody could see them, they set to work to make their little man.

The old husband insisted that it must be very small, and the old wife agreed that it should be almost as small as a new-born babe. Kneeling down in the snow, they fashioned the little body in next to no time. Now there remained only the head to finish. Two fat handfuls of snow for the cheeks and face, and a big one on top for the head. Then they put on a wee dab for the nose and poked two holes, one on each side, for the eyes.

It was soon done, and they were already standing back looking at it, and laughing and clapping their hands like children. Then suddenly they stopped. What had happened? A very strange thing indeed! Out of the two holes they saw looking at them two wistful blue eyes. Then the face of the little snow man was no longer white. The cheeks became rounded and smooth and radiant, and two rosy lips began to smile up at them. A breath of wind brushed the snow from the head, and it all fell down round the shoulders in flaxen ringlets escaping from a white fur cap. At the same time some snow, loosened from the little body, fell down and took the shape of a pretty white garment. Then, suddenly, before they could open and shut their mouths, their snow mannikin was gone, and in his place stood the daintiest, prettiest little maiden they had ever seen.

They gave each other a look out of the corners of their eyes, and scratched their heads in wonderment. But it was as true as true. There stood the little girl, all pink and white before them. She was really alive, for she ran to them; and, when they stooped down to lift her up, she put one arm round the old wife's neck and the other round the old man's, and gave them each a hug and a kiss.

They laughed and cried for joy; then, suddenly remembering how real some dreams can seem, they pinched each other in turn. Still they were not sure, for the pinches might have been a part of the dream. So, in fear lest they might wake and spoil the whole thing, they wrapped the little girl up quickly and hastened back home.

On the way they met the children, still playing round their snow man; and the snowballs with which they pelted them in the back were very real; but there again, the snowballs might have belonged to the dream. But when they were inside the house, and saw the inglenook, with the soup in the pot by the fire and the bundle of wood near by, and everything just as they had left it, they looked at each other with tears in their eyes and no longer feared that it was all a dream. In another minute there was a little white fur cap hanging on the corner of the mantelpiece and two little shoes drying by the fire, while the old wife took the little girl on her lap and crooned a lullaby over her.

The old man put his hand on his wife's shoulder and she looked up.

"Marusha!"

"Youshko!"

"At last we have a little girl! We made her out of the snow, so we will call her Snegorotchka."

The old wife nodded her head, and then they kissed each other. When they had all had supper, they went to bed, the old husband and wife feeling sure that they would wake early in the morning to find the child still with them. And they were not disappointed. There she was, sitting up between them, prattling and laughing. But she had grown bigger, and her hair was now twice as long as at first. When she called them "Little Father" and "Little Mother" they were so delighted that they felt like dancing as nimbly as they had in their young days. But, instead of dancing, they just kissed each other, and wept for joy.

That day they held a big feast. The old wife was busy all the morning cooking all kinds of dainties, while the old man went round the village and collected the fiddlers. All the boys and girls of the village were invited, and they ate and sang and danced and had a merry time till daybreak. As they went home, the girls all talked at once about how much they had enjoyed themselves, but the boys were very silent;—they were thinking of the beautiful Snegorotchka with the blue eyes and the golden hair.

Every day after that Snegorotchka played with the other children, and taught them how to make castles and palaces of snow, with marble halls and thrones and beautiful fountains. The snow seemed to let her do whatever she liked with it, and to build itself up under her tiny fingers as if it knew exactly what shape it was to take. They were all greatly delighted with the wonderful things she made; but when she showed them how to dance as the snowflakes do, first in a brisk whirl, and then softly and lightly, they could think of nothing else but Snegorotchka. She was the little fairy queen of the children, the delight of the older people, and the very breath of life to old Marusha and Youshko.

And now the winter months moved on. With slow and steady stride they went from mountain top to mountain top, around the circle of the sky-line. The earth began to clothe itself in green. The great trees, holding out their naked arms like huge babies waiting to be dressed, were getting greener and greener, and last year's birds sat in their branches singing this year's songs. The early flowers shed their perfume on the breeze, and now and then a waft of warm air, straying from its summer haunts, caressed the cheek and breathed a glowing promise in the ear. The forests and the fields were stirring. A beautiful spirit brooded over the face of nature;—spring was trembling on the leash and tugging to be free.

One afternoon Marusha was sitting in the inglenook stirring the soup and singing a mournful song, because she had never felt so full of joy. The old man Youshko had just brought in a bundle of wood and laid it on the hearth. It seemed just the same as on that winter's afternoon when they saw the children dancing round their snow man; but what made all the difference was Snegorotchka, the apple of their eye, who now sat by the window, gazing out at the green grass and the budding trees.

Youshko had been looking at her; he had noticed that her face was pale and her eyes a shade less blue than usual. He grew anxious about her.

"Are you not feeling well, Snegorotchka?" he asked.

"No, Little Father," she replied sadly. "I miss the white snow,—oh! so much; the green grass is not half as beautiful. I wish the snow would come again."

"Oh! yes; the snow will come again," replied the old man. "But don't you like the leaves on the trees and the blossoms and the flowers, my darling?"

"They are not so beautiful as the pure, white snow." And Snegorotchka shuddered.

The next day she looked so pale and sad that they were alarmed, and glanced at one another anxiously.

"What ails the child?" said Marusha.

Youshko shook his head and looked from Snegorotchka to the fire, and then back again.

"My child," he said at last, "why don't you go out and play with the others? They are all enjoying themselves among the flowers in the forest; but I've noticed you never play with them now. Why is it, my darling?"

"I don't know, Little Father, but my heart seems to turn to water when the soft warm wind brings the scent of the blossoms."

"But we will come with you, my child," said the old man. "I will put my arm about you and shield you from the wind. Come, we will show you all the pretty flowers in the grass, and tell you their names, and you will just love them,—all of them."

So Marusha took the pot off the fire, and then they all went out together, Youshko with his arm round Snegorotchka to shield her from the wind. But they had not gone far when the warm perfume of the flowers wafted to them on the breeze, and the child trembled like a leaf. They both comforted her and kissed her, and then they went on towards the spot where the flowers grew thickly in the grass. But, as they passed a clump of big trees, a bright ray of sunlight struck through like a dart and Snegorotchka put her hand over her eyes and gave a cry of pain.

They stood still and looked at her. For a moment, as she drooped upon the old man's arm, her eyes met theirs; and on her upturned face were swiftly running tears which sparkled in the sunlight as they fell. Then, as they watched her, she grew smaller and smaller, until, at last, all that was left of Snegorotchka was a little patch of dew shining on the grass. One tear-drop had fallen into the cup of a flower. Youshko gathered that flower—very gently—and handed it to Marusha without a word.

They both understood now. Their darling was just a little girl made of snow, and she had melted away in the warmth of the sunlight.

"The Ghost—a Christmas Frolic," illustration from 1814. SOURCE: LIBRARY OF CONGRESS.

PART 7
The Wild Side

Monsters, ghosts, dressing up like animals and straw men. Sounds perfectly fitting for Halloween, but Christmas? Not lately. However, throughout history, Christmas has been filled with supernatural beings, superstition, fortune-telling, and scaring the daylights out of ourselves. Let's take a haunted hike through the wild side of Christmases long, long ago.

SOURCE: DOROTHY SIEMENS.

CHAPTER 21

Monsters

Something Wicked This Way Comes

The jolly little Christmas elves we know today are merely watered-down versions of the elves of northern European folklore that they were derived from. Those creatures were devious and often threatening. What's more, many people *really* believed in them. In fact, an ancient book of medicine warns that if a horse is experiencing pain, an elf could be to blame.

Belief in monsters and evil spirits was once common, and so it's only natural that such belief would carry into the Christmas season.

In Iceland, the *Jólasveinar*, or "Yule Lads," were creatures that looked and acted a bit more like traditionally troublesome elves. They would break into houses in the dark of night and pull nasty pranks or worse. The Yule Lads are still around today, though their image has softened considerably. They're now mostly thought of as lovable rascals.

In Greek folklore, the *kallikantzaroi* were monsters who lived in the underworld all year, except during the twelve days of Christmas. That's when they came up to maraud and pillage, tormenting humans in ways large and small. People observed various safeguards against the *kallikantzaroi*, such as keeping the Yule log burning throughout the season. It was even said that a child born on Christmas Day was likelier than most to become a *kallikantzaros*. Parents could avoid this outcome by singeing the children's toenails—the better to prevent them from turning into claws.

Werewolves and Christmas have a long history together. According to beliefs in some parts of Europe, you needed to be on heightened alert for werewolves during the twelve days of Christmas. During that time, they were said to hunt for humans and animals. Some people in Poland and Germany also believed that a child born on Christmas Day was likelier to become a werewolf.

In parts of Europe, Christmas was seen as a time of increased activity for witches. In Norway, for example, it was considered wise to hide all brooms to avoid attracting witches to your house. Perchta was a witchlike figure from folklore who would punish disobedience in gruesome fashion. Sometimes known as the "Christmas witch" or even the "female Krampus," she is described as obsessed with household chores, despising laziness and untidiness. Those who had not scrubbed the house clean and finished the season's fiber spinning by Twelfth Night were susceptible to Perchta's wrath. She punished offenders by slitting their bellies open, removing their innards, and replacing them with straw and pebbles.

Illustration of Perchta, 1910. SOURCE: WIKIMEDIA COMMONS.

OF CHRISTMASES LONG, LONG AGO

THE *KALLIKANTZAROI*

Greek and Gruesome

The *kallikantzaroi* are in a class of their own among Christmas monsters. Their folklore is very vividly fleshed out, and they were a genuine cause for concern among Greek peasants during the twelve days of Christmas.

Though traditions varied by region, a common version was that these creatures spent most of their time in the underworld, damaging the tree thought to support the earth. But that tree was regenerated every year by the birth of Jesus Christ, sending the *kallikantzaroi* into a rage. And so they came up to earth seeking vengeance during the twelve days of Christmas.

Their appearance is the stuff of nightmares. According to Clement Miles's 1912 book, *Christmas Customs and Traditions: Their History and Significance*, "They are half-animal, half-human monsters, black, hairy, with huge heads, glaring red eyes, goats' or asses' ears, blood-red tongues hanging out, ferocious tusks, monkey's arms, and long curved nails, and commonly they have the foot of some beast."

While on earth, they would hide out during the day, but after sunset they began their rampage. They broke into homes through the chimneys and windows, causing all kinds of injury and property damage. In addition to keeping the Yule log burning, people took other preventative measures, such as marking the house door with a black cross on Christmas Eve, burning something with a strong smell, or leaving food outside the house. Finally, with the arrival of Epiphany on January 6, the *kallikantzaroi* scurried back underground, often hurried along by the village priest sprinkling holy water on people and their houses.

Theories abound as to where this legend came from. Were the tales of the *kallikantzaroi* simply a variation on existing werewolf and vampire legends? Or did the legend grow from peasants—perhaps a bit tipsy in their revels—confusing what they saw during the masquerades of the festival of Dionysus? Those masquerades, characterized by grotesque animal costumes and noisy partying, coincided with the twelve days of Christmas. Whatever their origins, their legacy is that of some of the most terrifying and gruesome monsters from Christmas past.

SOURCE: DOROTHY SIEMENS.

CHAPTER 22
The Mari Lwyd
Haunted Horse Play

Come with me to a village in the south of Wales. It's sometime in, oh, let's say the mid- to late 1700s. The Christmas season is upon us. We're cozy and warm in our little village home.

Suddenly, our ears prick up. There's a raucous ruckus coming up the street—a group of voices, shouting and laughing and singing off key. It grows louder as it approaches us, until finally . . . there's a knock at our door.

Well, I'm not answering that. *You do it*.

You open the door, and what to your wondering eyes should appear? It's a horse's skull propped up on a pole, like a giant and creepy version of a children's hobbyhorse toy. There are ribbons dangling from the skull, bulbs of some kind bulging from the eye sockets, and a large sheet draping over the pole and covering the person or persons carrying it.

You've just encountered the Mari Lwyd (or gray mare).

This weird Welsh tradition, possibly inspired by Norse mythology, grew out of pre-Christian wintertime observances. These observances included folklore and characters that embodied fears about the cold, dark, dangerous winter days ahead.

The Mari Lwyd is said to rise from the dead each season. She became part of the Welsh wassailing tradition at Christmastime. Wassailers dressed as the Mari Lwyd went door to door, singing and reciting verse in exchange for hospitality (see also BEGGING VISITS). And in case it doesn't go without saying, alcohol was almost always involved. As such, the Mari Lwyd was also known to get a bit mischievous, pulling pranks and chasing villagers through the streets.

She might have remained an obscure regional tradition had she not been described in *A Tour Through Part of North Wales, in the year 1798, and at Other Times*, a book published in 1800 by the Reverend J. Evans. (Yes, even though the Mari Lwyd is a tradition of South Wales, Evans included it in his book.) As recognition grew, other clergy weighed in, often describing it as "pagan" or "sinful"—which, of course, only made it all the more popular.

The tradition of the Mari Lwyd began to decline around the 1930s. But the twenty-first century has brought her new recognition and interest.

FESTIVE PHOTOS
Snappy Snapshots of the Mari Lwyd

Shortly before the Mari Lwyd tradition began to decline in the early 1930s, some examples were captured on camera. These images come from the Welsh village of Llangynwyd.

The Mari Lwyd at Llangynwyd, circa 1910.
SOURCE: WIKIMEDIA COMMONS.

The Mari Lwyd at Llangynwyd, circa 1904. SOURCE: WIKIPEDIA.

affirmative will appear the safest side of the question; the unreasonable credulity of the dark ages was undoubtedly a snare, and the extreme is equally so; the latter staggers the grand doctrine of the Soul's immortality, for those who deny there are spirits subsisting without bodies will, after that, with more difficulty believe the separate existence of their own.

Among superstitious or singular customs we remarked the following:—

On Christmas Eve, about three o'clock in the morning, most of the parishioners assemble in the church, and after prayers and a sermon, continue singing psalms and hymns till day-light, and if, through infirmity or age, any are disabled from attending, they have prayers at home, and carols on the Nativity; this act of devotion is called *plygan*, or the *cock-crowing*.

Another very singular custom, I never could learn the *rationale* of is, that of a man on new year's day, dressing himself in blankets and other trappings, with a factitious head like a horse, and a party attending him, knocking for admittance, this obtained, he runs about the room with an uncommon frightful noise, which the company quit in real or pretended fright; they soon recover, and by reciting a verse of some ancient cowydd, or, in default, paying a small gratuity, they gain admission. A similar custom is prevalent in the Highlands; *(Vid. Johnson,)* and, from Du Cange, we find it was a practice of Heathenism.*

* Ludi profani apud Ethnicos & Paganos solebant in Kalendis Januarii; belluarum, pecudum, & Vetularum, assumptis formis, huc

The first known mention of the Mari Lwyd in print, from *A Tour Through Part of North Wales.* SOURCE: INTERNET ARCHIVE.

SOURCE: DOROTHY SIEMENS.

CHAPTER 23
Skeklers
Supernatural Straw Creatures

What does a strawman have to do with Christmas? Nothing much . . . unless you celebrate the season in Shetland, an archipelago off the coast of Scotland. That's where you'll find a unique—and visually striking—folk custom during wintertime celebrations, including the twelve days of Christmas.

The tradition of "skekling" dates back to the Norse history of the islands. Skeklers were typically children and adolescents wearing cloth face masks and dressed in a skirt, cloak, and cone-shaped hat, all made of straw. The effect was somewhere between a grass hut come to life and a scarecrow turned inside out.

Skekling began as an ancient ritual to hasten the return to warmer weather and ensure a bountiful crop. In time, it was conducted on Halloween, Christmas, and Up Helly Aa, a fire festival held in January. Even the occasional wedding could see a band of skeklers.

So how exactly does one . . . skekle? By wearing the straw costume, skeklers were playing the part of a supernatural being. To complete the effect, they'd also alter their voices by speaking only while inhaling. One important part of the ritual was that skeklers would never reveal their true identities.

Traveling in a group led by a *skudler*, the skeklers would enter homes and perform a dance. They would then pass around a special sheepskin bag to collect food in return for the ritual (see also Begging Visits).

Sometimes, when visiting a farm, skeklers would announce their arrival by firing a gun into the air. A gunshot in response meant they were welcome. The Shetland version may have been an evolution of a similar idea found on the nearby Faroe Islands. In the Faroe version, the face masks were wooden and the costumes made of seaweed.

During the nineteenth century, the tradition gradually diminished as islanders became increasingly receptive to British customs and lifestyles. By the early twentieth century, skekling had all but disappeared.

HOGMANAY
Welcome to the Daft Days

Skeklers may be an obscure regional tradition that came and went. But Scotland has made some lasting contributions to the holiday season. We can thank the Scots for shortbread and "Auld Lang Syne"—and, of course, some of the world's best whiskey.

Less known to Americans but celebrated vigorously by Scots past and present is Hogmanay.

Back in the mid-sixteenth century, when the Calvinist Church gained power in Scotland, feast days like Christmas and Epiphany were deemed papist creations to be abolished. The Calvinists eventually got their way, and celebrating Christmas was subject to various punishments, including excommunication. For a long period, Scotland had the distinction of being the only Christian country that didn't officially observe Christmas.

But *unofficially* . . . that's another story.

Existing Christmas (and Yule and solstice) celebrations were simply pushed down the calendar to New Year in the form of Hogmanay. Nobody is really sure where the word comes from, though theories abound. But the celebration is effectively a substitute for Christmas, with gift giving, visits to family and friends (see First-Footing), and feasting.

Other Hogmanay traditions include opening house doors at midnight to let the old year out and the new year in and singing "Auld Lang Syne." For one obscure tradition from the days of old, we can look to a description published in Iowa's *Audubon Republican* newspaper in December 1911 (see opposite page).

Hogmanay originally referred to the last day of the year, but it later referred to New Year's Eve *and* Day. It belongs to a period of festivities not unlike the twelve days of Christmas, known as the Daft Days. These last from Christmas through Handsel Monday, the traditional gift-giving day on the first Monday of the New Year.

Today, Hogmanay is as large a celebration in Scotland as Christmas. And even though Christmas has been embraced in Scotland for generations, it wasn't made an official public holiday until 1958!

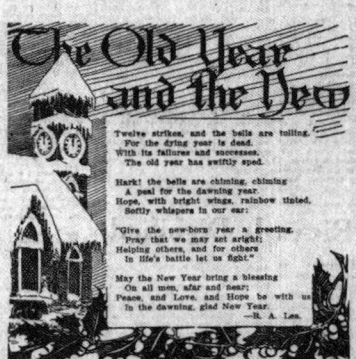

Article from Iowa's *Audubon Republican* newspaper describing Scottish Christmas traditions, 1911. SOURCE: LIBRARY OF CONGRESS.

SOURCE: DOROTHY SIEMENS.

CHAPTER 24
The Broad
Bullish on Christmas

Christmas isn't just the season of joy; it's also about tapping into that primal, animalistic energy. Back in the day, people didn't just deck the halls; some of them embraced their inner beasts. The tradition of sporting animal disguises during midwinter celebrations has its roots in pre-Christian customs. As Christianity took root across Europe, some of these ancient practices found new life as part of Christmas festivities, where they persisted into the late nineteenth and early twentieth centuries.

In many of these customs, people dressed as a horse or bull. In the quaint corners of the Cotswolds in south-central England, there was the curious custom known as "the Broad." Also known as "the Christmas Bull," it was a hobbyhorse with a bull's head perched atop a pole, carried by someone concealed beneath coarsely woven cloth. The Broad is one example of the "hooded animal" tradition observed with many regional variations throughout Britain and Ireland (see also THE MARI LWYD).

OF CHRISTMASES LONG, LONG AGO

The Broad probably grew out of earlier wassailing traditions. The costumed reveler was typically part of a wassailing group, going door to door with a band of followers. The goal was to be invited into homes, where the Broad would playfully imitate a threatening bull and receive some food and drink.

The bull's head itself could be a genuine taxidermized head, or an imitation made of cardboard or papier-mâché, or even, in some cases, a turnip or swede. It was often adorned with horns, glass eyes, and colorful ribbons.

A similar folk tradition from Kent in southeast England is known as "the hooden horse."

The Broad seems to have died out around the start of World War I. Unlike with the Mari Lwyd, though, no brave soul has yet attempted to resurrect the Broad . . . but who knows what the future holds?

THE BROAD

HOODED ANIMALS
A Curious Hobby (Horse)

The "hooded animal" tradition has existed in several regional flavors throughout England and Ireland. The Broad and Mari Lwyd are two variations on the same theme, though several others exist. The Old Horse, Old Ball, Old Tup, and the Hooden Horse are other examples of the same concept: a replica animal head mounted on a stick and held by a person covered in sackcloth.

Many of these customs were associated with Christmas, though Old Ball was associated with Easter. Most versions involved a horse's head, though Old Tup was a ram. Almost all versions involved a group of musicians and others accompanying the animal character on visits to homes and shops, where they would perform and expect a gratuity.

The exact origins of these folk customs are unclear, though they likely began in the sixteenth and seventeenth centuries. Many, like the Mari Lwyd, carried into the early twentieth century before fading away.

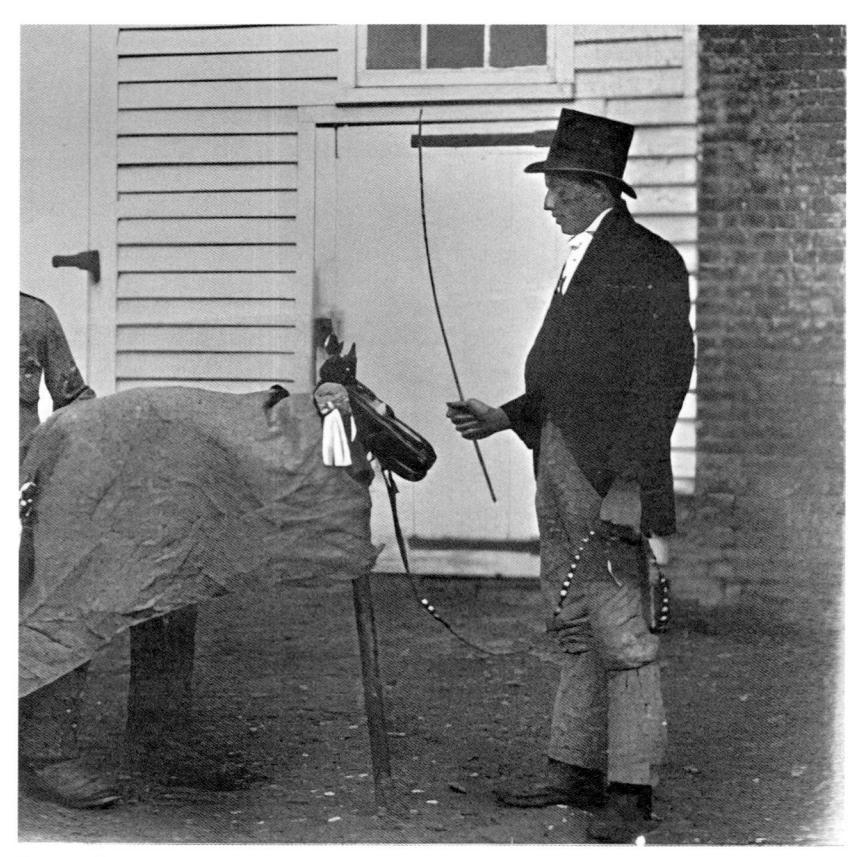

Photo from the 1909 book *The Hooden Horse* by Percy Maylam.
SOURCE: WIKIPEDIA.

Photo of Old Tup at Handsworth, taken pre-1907. SOURCE: WIKIPEDIA.

Photo from the 1909 book *The Hooden Horse* by Percy Maylam. SOURCE: WIKIPEDIA.

SOURCE: DOROTHY SIEMENS.

CHAPTER 25

Ghost Stories

We Wish You a Spooky Christmas

Christmas: It's the most wonderful time of the year, according to that song made famous by Andy Williams.

"There'll be parties for hosting..."

—*Sounds good... I'm with you so far*

"Marshmallows for toasting..."

—*Well, I do love a good toasted marshmallow*

"And caroling out in the snow..."

—*It wouldn't be Christmas without it*

"There'll be scary ghost stories and tales of the glories..."

—*Uh... say what, now? Scary ghost stories, did you say?*

These days, we're used to having only one of our holidays haunted by ghosts, and that holiday isn't Christmas. We tend to like our Christmases warm and cozy and to leave the spooky spectacle in the capable hands of Halloween.

OF CHRISTMASES LONG, LONG AGO

For the Victorians, however, Christmas Eve was a time to summon spirits from the beyond in the form of a good old-fashioned ghost story.

But . . . why?

Possibly the tradition grew out of pre-Christian winter celebrations that were steeped in folklore and superstition. Or maybe it was because Christmas gets us thinking about our departed loved ones. Or it could have come from the Victorians' intense cultural interest in ghosts. (Seances and spirit mediums were very much in vogue during that era.) Or maybe it was the explosive growth of print media during Victorian

Marley's ghost. Illustration by John Leech for the first edition of *A Christmas Carol*, 1843. SOURCE: WIKIMEDIA COMMONS.

times that allowed for ghost stories to be published and popularized. Or maybe it was a mix of spiked eggnog and cold, dark nights. The likely answer is that it was a combination of all of the above.

A Christmas Carol is by far the best-known published Christmas ghost story, but it's not the only one—not by a long shot. Heck, it's not even the only one that Charles Dickens wrote. And while *A Christmas Carol* does have multiple ghosts, it's not an especially scary ghost story. But other examples of the era (see below) do get seriously spooky.

We haven't altogether abandoned the idea of a creepy Christmas. Christmas slasher films, for example, attract a niche audience. So who knows? Maybe the Christmas ghost story will come back . . . from the dead.

SMEE
Hide and Shriek

Ready to gather 'round the fireplace and send shivers down the spines of your friends and family on Christmas Eve? You could make up your own ghost story, of course. But for an authentic experience, why not turn to the vast trove of classic creepy literature? "Smee," by A. M. Burrage, is a short story that first appeared in *Pall Mall Magazine* in 1929. It's a great example of the Victorian ghost story tradition, even though it was published years after the end of the Victorian era. Still, it takes place at a party on Christmas Eve and involves a chilling twist on a game of hide-and-seek. Best of all, it's genuinely spooky. Read on . . . if you dare!

SMEE

"No," said Jackson with a shy little smile. "I'm sorry. I won't play hide and seek."

It was Christmas Eve, and there were fourteen of us in the house. We had had a good dinner, and we were all in the mood for fun and games—all, that is, except Jackson. When somebody suggested hide and seek, there were loud shouts of agreement. Jackson's refusal was the only one.

It was not like Jackson to refuse to play a game. "Aren't you feeling well?" someone asked.

"I'm perfectly all right, thank you," he said. "But," he added with a smile that softened his refusal but did not change it, "I'm still not playing hide and seek."

"Why not?" someone asked. He hesitated for a moment before replying.

"I sometimes go and stay at a house where a girl was killed. She was playing hide and seek in the dark. She didn't know the house very well. There was a door that led to the servants' staircase. When she was chased, she thought the door led to a bedroom. She opened the door and jumped—and landed at the bottom of the stairs. She broke her neck, of course."

We all looked serious. Mrs Fernley said, "How terrible! And were you there when it happened?"

Jackson shook his head sadly. "No," he said, "but I was there when something else happened. Something worse."

"What could be worse than that?"

"This was," said Jackson. He hesitated for a moment, then he said, "I wonder if any of you have ever played a game called 'Smee.' It's much better than hide and seek. The name comes from 'It's me,' of course. Perhaps you'd like to play it instead of hide and seek. Let me tell you the rules of the game.

GHOST STORIES

"Every player is given a sheet of paper. All the sheets except one are blank. On the last sheet of paper is written 'Smee.' Nobody knows who 'Smee' is except 'Smee' himself—or herself. You turn out the lights, and 'Smee' goes quietly out of the room and hides. After a time the others go off to search for 'Smee'—but of course they don't know who they are looking for. When one player meets another he challenges him by saying, 'Smee.' The other player answers 'Smee,' and they continue searching.

"But the real 'Smee' doesn't answer when someone challenges. The second player stays quietly beside him. Presently they will be discovered by a third player. He will challenge and receive no answer, and he will join the first two. This goes on until all the players are in the same place. The last one to find 'Smee' has to pay a forfeit. It's a good, noisy, amusing game. In a big house it often takes a long time for everyone to find 'Smee.' Perhaps you'd like to try. I'll happily pay my forfeit and sit here by the fire while you play."

"It sounds a good game," I remarked. "Have you played it too, Jackson?"

"Yes," he answered. "I played it in the house that I was telling you about."

"And she was there? The girl who broke—."

"No, no," said someone else. "He told us he wasn't there when she broke her neck."

Jackson thought for a moment. "I don't know if she was there or not. I'm afraid she was. I know that there were thirteen of us playing the game, and there were only twelve people in the house. And I didn't know the dead girl's name. When I heard that whispered name in the dark, it didn't worry me. But I tell you, I'm never going to play that kind of game again. It made me quite nervous for a long time. I prefer to pay my forfeit at once!"

We all stared at him. His words did not make sense at all.

Tim Vouce was the kindest man in the world. He smiled at us all.

"This sounds like an interesting story," he said. "Come on, Jackson, you can tell it to us instead of paying a forfeit."

"Very well," said Jackson. And here is his story.

Have you met the Sangstons? They are cousins of mine, and they live in Surrey. Five years ago they invited me to go and spend Christmas with them. It was an old house, with lots of unnecessary passages and staircases. A stranger could get lost in it quite easily.

Well, I went down for that Christmas. Violet Sangston promised me that I knew most of the other guests. Unfortunately, I couldn't get away from my job until Christmas Eve. All the other guests had arrived there the previous day. I was the last to arrive, and I was only just in time for dinner. I said "Hullo" to everyone I knew, and Violet Sangston introduced me to the people I didn't know. Then it was time to go in to dinner.

That is perhaps why I didn't hear the name of a tall, darkhaired handsome girl whom I hadn't met before. Everyone was in rather a hurry and I am always bad at catching people's names. She looked cold and clever. She didn't look at all friendly, but she looked interesting, and I wondered who she was. I didn't ask, because I was sure that someone would speak to her by name during the meal. Unluckily, however, I was a long way from her at table. I was sitting next to Mrs Gorman, and as usual Mrs Gorman was being very bright and amusing. Her conversation is always worth listening to, and I completely forgot to ask the name of the dark, proud girl.

There were twelve of us, including the Sangstons themselves. We were all young—or trying to be young. Jack and Violet Sangston were the oldest, and their seventeen-year-old son Reggie was the youngest. It was Reggie who suggested "Smee" when the talk turned to games. He told us the rules of the game, just as I've described them to you. Jack Sangston warned us all. "If you are going to play games in the dark," he said, "please be careful of the back stairs on the first floor. A door leads to them, and I've often thought about taking the door off. In the dark a stranger to the house could think they were walking into a room. A girl really did break her neck on those stairs."

I asked how it happened.

"It was about ten years ago, before we came here. There was a party and they were playing hide and seek. This girl was looking for somewhere to hide. She heard somebody coming, and ran along the passage to get away. She opened the door, thinking it led to a bedroom. She planned to hide in there until the seeker had gone. Unfortunately it was the door that led to the back stairs. She fell straight down to the bottom of the stairs. She was dead when they picked her up."

We all promised to be careful. Mrs Gorman even made a little joke about living to be ninety. You see, none of us had known the poor girl, and we did not want to feel sad on Christmas Eve.

Well, we all started the game immediately after dinner. Young Reggie Sangston went round making sure all the lights were off, except the ones in the servants' rooms and in the sitting-room where we were. We then prepared twelve sheets of paper. Eleven of them were blank, and one of them had "Smee" written on it. Reggie mixed them all up, then we each took one.

The person who got the paper with "Smee" on it had to hide. I looked at mine and saw that it was blank. A moment later, all the electric lights went out. In the darkness I heard someone moving very quietly to the door.

After a minute somebody blew a whistle, and we all rushed to the door. I had no idea who was "Smee." For five or ten minutes we were all rushing up and down passages and in and out of rooms, challenging each other and answering, "Smee?—Smee!"

After a while, the noise died down, and I guessed that someone had found "Smee." After a time I found a group of people all sitting on some narrow stairs. I challenged, and received no answer. So "Smee" was

OF CHRISTMASES LONG, LONG AGO

there. I hurriedly joined the group. Presently two more players arrived. Each one was hurrying to avoid being last. Jack Sangston was last, and was given a forfeit.

"I think we're all here now, aren't we?" he remarked. He lit a match, looked up the staircase and began to count.

". . . Nine, ten, eleven, twelve, thirteen," he said, and then laughed. "That's silly—there's one too many!"

The match went out, and he lit another and began to count. He got as far as twelve, then he looked puzzled.

"There are thirteen people here!" he said. "I haven't counted myself yet."

"Oh, nonsense!" I laughed. "You probably began with yourself, and now you want to count yourself twice."

His son took out his electric torch. It gave a better light than the matches, and we all began to count. Of course there were twelve of us. Jack laughed. "Well," he said, "I was sure I counted thirteen twice."

From half way up the stairs Violet Sangston spoke nervously. "I thought there was somebody sitting two steps above me. Have you moved, Captain Ransome?"

The captain said that he hadn't. "But I thought there was somebody sitting between Mrs Sangston and me."

Just for a moment there was an uncomfortable something in the air. A cold finger seemed to touch us all. For that moment we all felt that something odd and unpleasant had just happened—and was likely to happen again. Then we laughed at ourselves, and at each other, and we felt normal again. There were only twelve of us, and that was that. Still laughing, we marched back to the sitting-room to begin again.

This time I was "Smee." Violet Sangston found me while I was searching for a hiding-place. That game didn't last long. Soon there were twelve people and the game was over. Violet felt cold, and wanted

160

her jacket. Her husband went up to their bedroom to fetch it. As soon as he'd gone, Reggie touched me on the arm. He was looking pale and sick. "Quick!" he whispered, "I've got to talk to you. Something horrible has happened."

We went into the breakfast-room. "What's the matter?" I asked.

"I don't know. You were 'Smee' last time, weren't you? Well, of course I didn't know who 'Smee' was. While Mother and the others ran to the west side of the house and found you, I went east. There's a deep clothes cupboard in my bedroom. It looked like a good hiding-place. I thought that perhaps 'Smee' might be there. I opened the door in the dark—and touched somebody's hand. 'Smee?' I whispered. There was no answer. I thought I'd found 'Smee.'

"Well, I don't understand it, but I suddenly had a strange, cold feeling. I can't describe it, but I felt that something was wrong. So I turned on my electric torch and there was nobody there.

"Now, I am sure I touched a hand. And nobody could get out of the cupboard, because I was standing in the doorway. What do you think?"

"You imagined that you touched a hand," I said.

He gave a short laugh. "I knew you would say that," he said. "Of course I imagined it. That's the only explanation, isn't it?"

I agreed with him. I could see that he still felt shaken. Together we returned to the sitting-room for another game of "Smee." The others were all ready and waiting to start again.

Perhaps it was my imagination (although I'm almost sure that it was not). But I had a feeling that nobody was really enjoying the game any more. But everyone was too polite to mention it. All the same, I had the feeling that something was wrong. All the fun had gone out of the game. Something deep inside me was trying to warn me. "Take care," it whispered. "Take care." There was some unnatural, unhealthy influence at work in the house. Why did I have this feeling? Because Jack

Sangston had counted thirteen people instead of twelve? Because his son imagined he had touched someone's hand in an empty cupboard? I tried to laugh at myself, but I did not succeed.

Well, we started again. While we were all chasing the unknown "Smee" we were all as noisy as ever. But it seemed to me that most of us were just acting. We were no longer enjoying the game. At first I stayed with the others. But for several minutes no "Smee" was found. I left the main group and started searching on the first floor at the west side of the house. And there, while I was feeling my way along, I bumped into a pair of human knees.

I put out my hand and touched a soft, heavy curtain. Then I knew where I was. There were tall, deep windows with window-seats at the end of the passage. The curtains reached to the ground. Somebody was sitting in a corner of one of the window-seats, behind a curtain.

"Aha!" I thought, "I've caught 'Smee'!" So I pulled the curtain to one side—and touched a woman's arm.

It was a dark, moonless night outside. I couldn't see the woman sitting in the corner of the window-seat.

"Smee?" I whispered.

There was no answer. When "Smee" is challenged, he—or she—does not answer. So I sat down beside her to wait for the others. Then I whispered, "What's your name?"

And out of the darkness beside me the whisper came: "Brenda Ford."

I did not know the name, but I guessed at once who she was. I knew every girl in the house by name except one. And that was the tall, pale, dark girl. So here she was sitting beside me on the window-seat, shut in between a heavy curtain and a window. I was beginning to enjoy the game. I wondered if she was enjoying it too. I whispered one or two rather ordinary questions to her, and received no answer.

"Smee" is a game of silence. It is a rule of the game that "Smee" and the person or persons who have found "Smee" have to keep quiet.

This, of course, makes it harder for the others to find them. But there was nobody else about. I wondered, therefore, why she was insisting on silence. I spoke again and got no answer. I began to feel a little annoyed. "Perhaps she is one of those cold, clever girls who have a poor opinion of all men," I thought. "She doesn't like me, and she is using the rules of the game as an excuse for not speaking. Well, if she doesn't like sitting here with me, I certainly don't want to sit with her!" I turned away from her.

"I hope someone finds us soon," I thought.

As I sat there, I realized that I disliked sitting beside this girl very much indeed. That was strange. The girl I had seen at dinner had seemed likeable in a cold kind of way. I noticed her and wanted to know more about her. But now I felt really uncomfortable beside her. The feeling of something wrong, something unnatural, was growing. I remembered touching her arm, and I trembled with horror. I wanted to jump up and run away. I prayed that someone else would come along soon.

Just then I heard light footsteps in the passage. Somebody on the other side of the curtain brushed against my knees. The curtain moved to one side, and a woman's hand touched my shoulder. "Smee?" whispered a voice that I recognized at once. It was Mrs Gorman. Of course she received no answer. She came and sat down beside me, and at once I felt very much better.

"It's Tony Jackson, isn't it?" she whispered.

"Yes," I whispered back.

"You're not 'Smee,' are you?"

"No, she's on my other side."

She reached out across me. I heard her finger-nails scratch a woman's silk dress.

"Hullo, 'Smee.' How are you? Who are you? Oh, is it against the rules to talk? Never mind, Tony, we'll break the rules. Do you know,

Tony, this game is beginning to annoy me a little. I hope they aren't going to play it all evening. I'd like to play a nice quiet game, all together beside a warm fire."

"Me too," I agreed.

"Can't you suggest something to them? There's something rather unhealthy about this particular game. I'm sure I'm being very silly. But I can't get rid of the idea that we've got an extra player . . . somebody who ought not to be here at all."

That was exactly how I felt, but I didn't say so. However, I felt very much better. Mrs Gorman's arrival had chased away my fears. We sat talking. "I wonder when the others will find us?" said Mrs Gorman.

After a time we heard the sound of feet, and young Reggie's voice shouting, "Hullo, hullo! Is anybody there?"

"Yes," I answered.

"Is Mrs Gorman with you?"

"Yes."

"What happened to you? You've both got forfeits. We've all been waiting for you for hours."

"But you haven't found 'Smee' yet," I complained.

"You haven't, you mean. I was 'Smee' this time."

"But 'Smee' is here with us!" I cried.

"Yes," agreed Mrs Gorman.

The curtain was pulled back and we sat looking into the eye of Reggie's electric torch. I looked at Mrs Gorman, and then on my other side. Between me and the wall was an empty place on the window-seat. I stood up at once. Then I sat down again. I was feeling very sick and the world seemed to be going round and round.

"There was somebody there," I insisted, "because I touched her."

"So did I," said Mrs Gorman, in a trembling voice. "And I don't think anyone could leave this window-seat without us knowing."

GHOST STORIES

Reggie gave a shaky little laugh. I remembered his unpleasant experience earlier that evening. "Someone's been playing jokes," he said. "Are you coming down?"

We were not very popular when we came down to the sitting-room.

"I found the two of them sitting behind a curtain, on a window-seat," said Reggie.

I went up to the tall, dark girl.

"So you pretended to be 'Smee,' and then went away!" I accused her.

She shook her head. Afterwards we all played cards in the sitting-room, and I was very glad.

Some time later, Jack Sangston wanted to talk to me. I could see that he was rather cross with me, and soon he told me the reason.

"Tony," he said, "I suppose you are in love with Mrs Gorman. That's your business, but please don't make love to her in my house, during a game. You kept everyone waiting. It was very rude of you, and I'm ashamed of you."

"But we were not alone!" I protested. "There was somebody else there—somebody who was pretending to be 'Smee.' I believe it was that tall, dark girl, Miss Ford. She whispered her name to me. Of course, she refused to admit it afterwards."

Jack Sangston stared at me. "Miss who?" he breathed.

"Brenda Ford, she said."

Jack put a hand on my shoulder. "Look here, Tony," he said, "I don't mind a joke, but enough is enough. We don't want to worry the ladies. Brenda Ford is the name of the girl who broke her neck on the stairs. She was playing hide and seek here ten years ago."

Acknowledgments

A Christmas book, like Christmas itself, is a family affair. I'm grateful to have been surrounded by many people whose support and contributions made this book possible. First, I'd like to thank Eric Myers, my literary agent, for being the first reader and cheerleader of my ideas and helping me turn them into viable concepts. I'm forever grateful for your encouragement, guidance, and tenacity. A very big thanks to Dorothy Siemens for the wonderful original illustrations that appear in this book. When I dreamed up the concept for *Of Christmases Long, Long Ago*, I had her illustrations in mind. I'm thrilled that we had the chance to work together on this project. So much of what I know about Christmas, I learned from Gerry Bowler's writings. A dog-eared copy of *The World Encyclopedia of Christmas* sits above my desk and serves as a constant reference. Gerry has been a repeat guest on *Christmas Past*, and I'm indebted to him for the wonderful foreword he contributed to this book. Many thanks also go to Alex Palmer, Jeff Belanger, Mark Voger, and Thomas Ruys Smith. I'm grateful to them for their comradery and creative inspiration and for sharing their thoughts on this book. A big thank-you to everyone at Lyons Press, especially Rick Rinehart,

Patricia Stevenson, Piper Wallis, and Rhonda Baker. As always, I must also thank all the listeners of *Christmas Past*, without whom none of this would be possible. And finally to my wife, Christine, and son, Dashiell, for their love and Christmas spirit, and for all the Christmas memories created and yet to come.

About the Author and Illustrator

Brian Earl is the host of *Christmas Past*, the hit podcast that tells the fascinating stories behind Christmas traditions. *Christmas Past* has appeared on the History Channel and NPR and in *Time*, *People*, *Vanity Fair*, *Saturday Evening Post*, *Newsweek*, and elsewhere. Brian lives in California with his wife and son. This is his second book.

Dorothy Siemens is an illustrator and printmaker based in Portland, Oregon. Her work is an exploration of form and color, drawing on warm textured shapes, bold colors, and spirited (but casual) actors to weave atmospheric stories. Her work has appeared in publications such as *Mother Jones* and the *New York Times*.